T0271408

International Trade and the Music Industry

Live music events are synonymous with fun but seldom associated with international trade. This book serves to transform this mindset, through describing the economic value of live music and analysing the factors affecting international trade in Caribbean live music services.

Race and ethnicity, unachieved regionalism within the Caribbean, and perceived biases in international trade agreements are assessed in relation to their impact on this trade. Several topics presented in this book are based on empirical findings from a previous microeconomic study, dedicated entirely to international trade in live music. Moreover, this book is unique because it compares the Caribbean and South Korea to assess the effectiveness of strategies aimed at developing international trade in live music services. This comparison should inspire robust policy initiatives for advancing international trade in Caribbean live music, given that South Korea is presently a heavyweight in the export of its entertainment services, despite language barriers.

Given the interdisciplinary nature of this book, it will appeal to a wide range of readers such as postgraduate students or researchers of microeconomics, intraregional trade, international trade, international business, international relations, public policy, and cultural studies, as well as IP legal professionals, live music stakeholders, cultural practitioners, and policymakers.

Lisa Gordon earned a PhD in International Relations with a specialty in International Trade from the University of the West Indies, St Augustine, Trinidad and Tobago. Dr. Gordon also received a master's degree in International Business and Foreign Languages from the Université Lumiere, Lyon 2, France. As a multilingual researcher, her expertise in international trade and international business has been sought by the Regional Council of Guadeloupe, the Université Rennes, France as well as French business consultancy firm ADEA-EURAFRIC Partners.

Routledge Studies in the Economics of Business and Industry

For more information about this series, please visit www.routledge.
com/Routledge-Studies-in-the-Economics-of-Business-and-Industry/
book-series/RSEBI

International Trade and the Music Industry

Live Music Services from the Caribbean

Lisa Gordon

Routledge
Taylor & Francis Group

LONDON AND NEW YORK

First published 2023
by Routledge
4 Park Square, Milton Park, Abingdon, Oxon OX14 4RN

and by Routledge
605 Third Avenue, New York, NY 10158

Routledge is an imprint of the Taylor & Francis Group, an informa business

British Library Cataloguing-in-Publication Data
A catalogue record for this book is available from the British Library

Library of Congress Cataloging-in-Publication Data
Names: Gordon, Lisa, author.
Title: International trade and the music industry : live music services from the Caribbean / Lisa Gordon.
Description: [1.] | Abingdon, Oxon ; New York : Routledge, 2023. | Series: Routledge studies in the economics of business and industry | Includes bibliographical references and index.
Identifiers: LCCN 2022044778 | ISBN 9781032380612 (hardback) | ISBN 9781032380636 (paperback) | ISBN 9781003343325 (ebook)
Subjects: LCSH: Music trade—Caribbean Area. | Caribbean Area—Commerce. | Concerts—Economic aspects. | International trade. | Music trade—Korea (South)
Classification: LCC ML3790 .G667 2023 |
DDC 780/.0382—dc23/eng/20221116
LC record available at https://lccn.loc.gov/2022044778

ISBN: 978-1-032-38061-2 (hbk)
ISBN: 978-1-032-38063-6 (pbk)
ISBN: 978-1-003-34332-5 (ebk)

DOI: 10.4324/9781003343325

Typeset in Times New Roman
by codeMantra

Contents

Foreword

The effects of the way society lives are visible like never before. Technology beams into our houses, and we can all see the reports of climate change from Asia to Europe to Africa to the Americas. Technology also has changed for international trade and music, and that is the focus of this timely book. As the world has faced the challenges of COVID-19 and resulting economic recession, it is welcome to have interdisciplinary research on how economic development can happen through trade and music.

The book focuses on international trade and music and the reconceptualisation of this activity as a vehicle for economic development. The geographical scope is on the Caribbean, and this is a highlight as more interdisciplinary research on this region is needed. That this book has this focus signifies its originality, and for me that makes it an enjoyable and impressive read. I am sure many will find this an interesting, insightful, and well-written text.

Particular and notable research analysis of value is contained within the book, which I am sure will prove itself in the longevity of the research conclusions. The researcher has taken time to define live music and explore the dimensions of its economic value. A range of characteristics are analysed from culture, race, strategy, trade failure, technology, and law and how they affect live music and its economic value internationally. The coverage of many of these issues and to do so with a collective interdisciplinary lens is impressive.

Overall, for me, this research offers originality and emphasises pathways of how countries can proceed and have their music sector contribute to socio-economic development. The researcher has opened the door to many possible avenues of future research. I think a whole range of economic stakeholders will be very interested in the results, and this book could have real-world impact. The author should be commended for her time, perspiration, and perseverance which has enabled her to introduce us to a compelling account of how music, culture, and experience engage with economic trade across the world and specifically the Caribbean.

Raphael J Heffron, Trinidad & Tobago, 31 August 2022

Raphael J Heffron BA, MA, MLitt, MPhil, MSc, PhD, Barrister-at-Law
Professor of Global Energy Law & Sustainability
EU Jean Monnet Professor in the Just Transition to a Low-Carbon Economy (2019–22) - Senior Counsel @ Janson, Brussels, Belgium
Senior Fellow of the UK Higher Education Academy – Fellow of the Royal Society of Arts – Fellow of the Royal Society of Edinburgh's Young Academy of Scotland
Visiting Professor ESCP Business School (London, Paris & Madrid), Université Paris-Dauphine (France), Queen Mary University of London, Eduardo Mondlane University (Mozambique), University of Brawijaja (Indonesia), University of Western Australia and Associate Researcher, Energy Policy Research Group, University of Cambridge (UK) & Oxford Institute for Energy Studies (UK)

Preface

Why Live Music Trade?

In the early stages of preparing this book, misgivings were expressed that the specificity of the topic of live music trade might be too narrow and that the contribution to the big picture side of things might be limited. While these concerns were certainly noted and appreciated, I also considered that there have been numerous sector-specific trade studies on non-cultural services that have been published. There are, for instance, many sector-specific studies in trade in transport services such as air carrier services or cruise-line services. Similarly, there have been numerous trade studies published on niche energy services. Studies of LNG production services or renewable energy services come to mind. Given the high number of publications on studies of this nature, arguably, questions on their narrowness in scope might have never come into play. And so, having weighed the doubts raised about my chosen topic along with my own anecdotal observation, I have concluded that the misgivings expressed are symptomatic of a pervasive problem within the world of economic research: The unfortunate reflex of underestimating the economic contribution of cultural services. This book, therefore, will hopefully transform the global psyche on specialised trade studies on cultural services like live music. If specialised, international trade studies are good for energy or transport services sectors, then I proffer, they are certainly good for the creative and cultural services sector. Moreover, the decision to focus specifically on live music trade was borne out of pure necessity. I saw an alarming paucity in refereed books on international trade and the music industry and especially, international trade in live music services. This I found rather surprising, given the economic importance of live music in supporting livelihoods. In the United Kingdom, for example, live music was said to account for 30,000 jobs in 2019 (Music by Numbers 2019). In France, in 2012 live music accounted for 375,239 jobs (L'hermite and Perrin 2012). In addition to supporting livelihoods, evidence suggests that live music services are sources of foreign exchange. Recently, the legendary Swedish group ABBA, for their worldwide ABBA Voyage reunion tour, garnered 380,000 in ticket sales within the first few days of their 2022–2023 UK residency, despite the astronomical ticket cost range of up to 474 pounds! In South Korea, live music appears to be a significant income generator. Apart from drawing scores of domestic ticket sales, live K-pop bands have lucrative export markets for their live music services in China and Japan as well as North America, Latin America, and Europe. Surely, with such examples, one can understand the absolute necessity of a book dedicated to the international trade in live music services.

Why Specific Focus on International Trade in Caribbean Live Music Services?

When this book was just an idea, some feared that the geographical focus of the book, which is on the live music services from the Caribbean, might render it narrow. They gave no arguments in support of their opinion. Consequentially, I was left to deduce that like the case of cultural services industries, there appears to be an unconscious bias towards undervaluing the global relevance of studies about the Caribbean, even if Caribbean researchers find them highly relevant to one's understanding of the world. If my deduction is the case, this is unfortunate. This is because the Caribbean is a region more than its sun, sea, sand, and its cliched "bananas". It is equally a regional heavyweight in terms of its global contribution to intellectual thought, public service, and culture. In contemporary intellectual thought and public service, there are the likes of Barbadian Prime Minister Mia Mottley, a committed advocate on climate change who was, in 2022, featured on the cover of Time magazine's top 100 influential people of the world issue. Similarly, United States, vice president Kamala Harris, of half-Jamaican ancestry, became the first woman vice president of that country, again representing the Caribbean's contribution to global public service. The late Saint Lucian economist, Sir Arthur Lewis, a Nobel laureate, is recognised the world over for his economic models which have been applied as far as Southeast Asia, just as Trinidad's first prime minister and economic historian, the late Dr. Eric Williams, has been internationally valued for his analysis on the effects of colonialism in a post-colonial society.

Furthermore, in terms of culture, and quite specifically music, the region has, for centuries, made an enormous contribution to the global musical landscape. These contributions are incarnated through artistes such as the prolific Jamaican musical prodigy, Bob Marley, whose recorded live reggae performances continue to be revered today and transcend generations and cultures. Similarly, calypso and steelpan music which have their origins in Trinidad & Tobago, have, for centuries, inspired the global music scene as can be seen in some old Hollywood films as clearly shown with the American group, The Andrews Sisters who rose to fame with their cover of the calypso "Rum n Coca-Cola". I am almost certain, had intellectual property rights been monitored in those days to the degree that they are currently, Trinidadian Rupert "Lord Invader" Grant who wrote the lyrics to "Rum n Coca-Cola", might have died as a rich man rather than as a struggling artiste. Likewise, the people of Martinique might have also monetarily benefitted from the popularity of this song, had intellectual property rights been properly enforced in those days. The musical score of 'Rum n' Coca-Cola was lifted from an old Martiniquan folk song, "L'année passée".

The high quality and international demand for Caribbean music is also embodied by the late legendary Guadeloupean singer and bass guitarist, Jacob Desvarieux of the overseas French Caribbean band Kassav'. His live zouk music crossed and continues to cross borders, cultures, and generations. And, if there were any further misgivings about the Caribbean region being too limited in geographical scope for an examination of live music trade, the meteoric success of Barbadian Rihanna, Trinidadians Nicki Minaj, and Broadway musical star Heather Headley as well as Jamaican live performers Shaggy and Sean Paul are just but a few examples of the world class quality and international demand for live music services from the Caribbean. Surely, a refereed book on international trade in live music from this region, which is bursting with creative talent, is certainly required and long overdue!

Who Is This Book For?

This book's interdisciplinary approach to the study of live music trade is what makes it such an interesting and informative read. Although it is a book framed within international trade theory, it also offers a wide spectrum of topics which would appeal to students and academics covering other fields such as international relations, environmental issues, race & ethnicity, culture, and research methods. Each chapter looks at these issues within the context of Caribbean live music trade, comparing where necessary the Caribbean context with the live music trade environment of other regions of the world. It also looks at how a multilateral institution, such as the World Trade Organisation (WTO), can play a role in the development of international trade in Caribbean live music services.

This book is also interesting for those who have always been curious about the Caribbean perspective on its trade matters with the North as well as Caribbean interregional trade. In this book, discussions from Caribbean scholars on how Caribbean regionalism and North-South preferential trade arrangements are impacting on trade outcomes will be examined for the purpose of theorising on how these outcomes could impact on interregional trade in Caribbean live music services.

The value of this book also resides in its easy-to-follow proposal of a research method for further studies on trade in Caribbean live music services and perhaps live music services of other regions of the world. This is especially true if you are a social scientist, economist, or international trade specialist in search of an empirical research design template that can be used for a sector-specific study on cultural services trade, for which data are scarce. The book presents an easy-to-follow experimental research design not dependent on data sets which have been collected overtime.

Lastly, if you are an interested policymaker looking for concrete solutions to develop international trade in cultural services, your needs will be met in this book. You will find, for example, chapters which comparatively assess the programmes and policies within East Asia's booming entertainment export industry to see if they would be applicable to the context of international trade in Caribbean live music services.

There are lots to be digested in this book, happy reading!

Acknowledgements

In addition to all the live music stakeholders and trade specialists whom I interviewed, I would like to sincerely thank the following:

Anthony P. Gonzales (PhD), The University of the West Indies, St Augustine, Trinidad

Keith Nurse (PhD) Sir Arthur Lewis Community College, St Lucia

Patrick K. Watson (Prof. Emeritus), The University of the West Indies, St Augustine, Trinidad

Alain Maurin (Prof.) Université des Antilles, Guadeloupe

Fred Reno (Prof.) Université des Antilles, Guadeloupe

Julien Merion, CORECA, Guadeloupe

Rodolphe Robin (PhD) Université Rennes 2, Brittany, France

Ruidy Vardarassin, Deputy Director, Ville de Baie-Mahault, Guadeloupe

Acronyms and Abbreviations

ACP	Organisation of African Caribbean Pacific States
ACS	Association of Caribbean States
CARICOM	Caribbean Community
EPA	Economic Partnership Agreement
EU	European Union
OECS	Organisation of Eastern Caribbean States
WTO	World Trade Organisation

1 The Basics of Live Music Services Trade

What Is Interregional Trade

Interregional trade refers to trade between or among regions. Therefore, trade in Caribbean live music services between the European Union and the CARIFORUM (a regional trading bloc comprised of 16 independent Caribbean countries) is classified as interregional trade. Similarly, live music services trade within the CARIFORUM regional trading bloc can also be defined as being interregional. This is because this trading bloc is comprised of individual Caribbean states where some have a common currency and others their own currency.

What Is Intraregional Trade

Interregional trade is at times classified into two categories: intraregional and extra-regional. Intraregional trade refers to trade which is localised in a specific geographical zone among countries which are characterised by the following:

- a common political system such as what occurs with Commonwealth Caribbean countries which follow the Westminster system of governance and/or;
- the use of a common currency and/or;
- belong to common regional blocs and/or single market regimes. Trade among most Caribbean states, for example, which belong to the Organisation of Eastern Caribbean States (OECS) and the Caribbean Community (CARICOM) could arguably be classified as intraregional. The term "arguably" is used here because within these regional blocs there are non-sovereign Caribbean territories which use extra-regional currency such as the Euro and

DOI: 10.4324/9781003343325-1

are geopolitically under the governing jurisdiction of European metropoles (e.g. Martinique and Guadeloupe).

To facilitate intraregional trade, trading blocs are usually created with the intention of harmonising laws, currencies, human resource, and data sharing among countries that are located within the same geographical space. Within the Caribbean, the CARICOM has been working towards establishing the Caribbean Single Market Economy (CSME) as a mechanism for facilitating trade within this regional community. Therefore, it is reasonable to conclude that the CARICOM can be classified as a regional trading bloc which has an intraregional trade mandate. The European Union is possibly the best reference of a regional bloc that has successfully facilitated intraregional trade within nations located in the same region (Europe). Intraregional trade can also mean domestic trade among states, provinces, or regional departments within a country, even if these states, provinces, or departments are situated in different geographical locations. Therefore, trade between France and its overseas territories of the Caribbean will still be classified as intraregional trade even though the geographic distance between them is great.

What Is Extra-Regional Trade

Extra-regional trade, however, relates to trade that is not localised within a given geographic region or country. And so, live music trade between the English-speaking independent Caribbean countries of the CARIFORUM and European Union countries, such as Belgium, would be classified as extra-regional trade. Similarly, trade between the French Overseas Caribbean territories and Canada or the United States could be considered as extra-regional.

What Is South-South Trade

The term "South" refers to countries which are situated between the tropics of Cancer and Capricorn. Many experts proffer that most developing nations are found in this geographical location. Therefore, international trade among countries within this geographical location is called South-South trade. And so, live music services trade between the English-speaking CARIFORUM countries and the overseas French Caribbean territories, though extra-regional (because of the geopolitical and currency differences between them), can still be defined as South-South trade. Some might argue that because the French overseas territories are satellites of France, that they ought to be classified as developed and consequently territories which represent the North. However, the reality is that many of these overseas French Caribbean territories suffer similar development issues like their neighbouring independent Caribbean nations which are classified as developing states of the South. Some of these shared socio-economic development issues include inferior health services, high rates of unemployment, poverty, delinquency, and lacking infrastructure especially in relation to water resources and energy (Taglioni 1997). Therefore, in this book, live music services trade between the overseas Caribbean territories of the European Union and the CARIFORUM states will be classified as South-South interregional trade which is extra-regional in nature.

What Is North-South Trade

The "North" in international trade terms refers to countries which are located in temperate zones. It is argued that most of the prosperous nations are found within this location.[1] Therefore, live music services trade between the United Kingdom and the CARIFORUM will be defined as North-South interregional trade which is extra-regional in nature. Similarly, live music services trade between the overseas French Caribbean territories and the United States can be described as North-South interregional trade which is also extra-regional in nature.

What Is a Service

A service is an intangible or immaterial product which carries economic value. It is differentiated from goods which are tangible or material products which carry monetary value. Examples of services include those of culture such as live music, entertainment streaming platforms, as well as commercial tours to art galleries and museums. Restaurant catering is also a service which carries both cultural and monetary value. Other non-cultural services which are monetised include financial services (off-shore banking, insurance), air-transport, taxi services, information technology (IT) services, education services (online/face to face) as well as technical and/or consulting services in fields such as energy or law.

What Are the Four Modes of Trade in Services?

The World Trade Organization (WTO) has defined four modes via which services are traded.[2] These four modes of trade are classified under the General Accord of Trade in Services (GATS). They are as follows:

1. Cross-border Trade
2. Consumption Abroad
3. Commercial Presence
4. Movement of Natural Persons

Mode 1 – Cross-border trade – This concerns services which are traded via cable, satellite, or ICT. In the case of live music, live concerts which are streamed via commercial online platforms are examples of cross-border exchange.

   Mode 2 – Consumption Abroad – This refers to travelling to consume a service. Relative to live music services, concertgoers from Europe who travel to the Caribbean to attend music festivals which they have paid for, are an example of consumption abroad.

   Mode 3 – Commercial (physical) Presence – Services traded via this mode require that foreign businesses have physical establishments within a host country. The act of Caribbean music producers setting up branches of their recording studios in the EU, would constitute commercial presence.

   Mode 4 – Movement of Natural Persons –- This refers to service providers travelling to another country to deliver a service. An artiste or live performer from Europe who does a concert tour in the Caribbean would be trading his services via this mode.

The Relevance of the Four Modes on Trade in Live Music Services

Customarily, live music services are traded via mode 4 (touring of artistes) and mode 2 (tourist travel to festivals). Mode 4 (touring), for example, is an important source of revenue for live performers from the English-speaking Caribbean. It is estimated that 95 percent of the earnings of Caribbean performers comes from touring. The importance of mode 4 (touring) would appear to be a universal norm. British live performer Sir Elton John following BREXIT expressed concerns over the impact that the current denial of British access to borderless travel into the EU, would have on the livelihoods of emerging artistes in his country (Savage 2021).

Despite the importance of this mode of trade, data capture on the volume of trade via this mode seems to be a universal dilemma. In the Caribbean, there is barely any published data on how much mode 4 (touring) contributes to the local economy of the region. (Data capture challenges are discussed in further detail in the book.) The international nature of this problem is underscored by the recently published (UK Music 2021) report. The report, though providing general information on how the British music industry fared in terms of its GVA contribution for the period 2019, notably did not provide any information on the value of touring (mode 4). This, therefore, arguably, suggests that like the Caribbean, the nations of the North are also experiencing challenges in compiling data of this kind.

Relative to travel to festivals/concerts (mode 2), this is also the other major means through which live music is traded. Estimates on the contribution made via this mode seem more easily accessible, with statisticians and other researchers depending on visitor arrival and hotel occupancy data and/or venue capacity ticket sales to make an overall estimate of the value of festival visits within a country.

Summary of Chapters

Chapter 1 – Introduction: The Basics of Live Music Services Trade

This is the foundational chapter. It explains international trade terminology and how they relate to trade in live music services. Terms such as interregional, intraregional, and extra-regional trade as well as descriptions about what is a service and the four modes through which services are exchanged are addressed in this chapter. This chapter prepares one to fully understand the discussions which will follow in the other chapters.

Chapter 2 – The Economic Importance of Live Music Services

This chapter illustrates the relevance of this book's topic. It does this by situating Caribbean live music services within both an international and a regional context.

Chapter 3 – Regionalism, International Trade Policy, and Caribbean Live Music Services

This chapter illustrates why empirical studies on trade in Caribbean live music services are needed. This is because it cites the problems faced in the development of Caribbean live music services by presenting the arguments of Caribbean scholars who proffer that the unachieved goal of South-South regionalism and, arguably, biased North-South international trade policies are among the root causes for the lack of development of trade in Caribbean services. The chapter, therefore, provides food for thought on the key causes of the problems impacting on international trade in Caribbean live music services that might require future experimental studies.

Chapter 4 – Introduction to Experimental Studies on International Trade and the Music Industry

This chapter proposes a research design for further empirical studies aimed at exploring what are the current problems affecting trade in Caribbean live music services. The proposed research design is inspired by an original research approach which was used for a study on live music services trade between European Union French Caribbean territories and Independent Anglophone CARIFORUM countries. The research design with the aid of illustrations will present a step-by-step approach to how to embark on scientific studies on live music services. Presenting this approach is particularly important for offering an alternative argument to the view held by certain Caribbean quarters that cultural services such as live music services cannot and should not be approached using the paradigm of international trade theory and statistical modelling, as happens with non-cultural services.

Chapter 5 – When Trade Facilitation Fails: Adopting the K-pop Export Approach to Caribbean Live Music

This chapter presents findings from a study on interregional trade in Caribbean live music which showed that trade facilitation measures were not having a satisfactory impact on this trade. Therefore, it considers whether South Korea's export strategy for its live music could be applied to South-South and North-South interregional trade in Caribbean live music services. To this end, arguments examining the usefulness of integrating the region's international relations priorities with an export strategy to develop international trade in Caribbean live music will also be presented in this chapter. This chapter also discusses the role that the WTO can play in facilitating international trade in Caribbean live music services.

Chapter 6 – Overcoming Cultural Issues in International Trade in Caribbean Live Music: The K-pop Strategy

This chapter proposes strategic solutions to addressing the negative impact of cultural issues on interregional trade in live music services. It does this by drawing from South Korea's music industry experience and comparing it to the Caribbean context.

Chapter 7 – Race & Ethnicity and International Trade in Caribbean Live Music: Why Exploring This Nexxus Is Important

This chapter suggests that further studies on international trade in Caribbean live music services include an investigation on the effects of race and ethnicity on this trade. It does so by referencing examples of how race and ethnicity might be factoring into how live performers of the Caribbean are faring in trading their services in the North.

Chapter 8 – Implications of Technology, Legal Institutions, and Geographic Proximity in the Development of Trade in Caribbean Live Music

This final chapter fulfils one need with three deeds. It looks at how technology, legal institutions, and geographic proximity can be harnessed for the development of interregional trade in Caribbean live music services. The proposals proffered on technology are inspired by South Korea's K-pop live music stakeholders who have used technology for the advancement of their trade in services to both intraregional and extra-regional markets. Conversely, the section on legal institutions explores how existing projects aimed at harmonising various commercial legal frameworks in the Caribbean can be used for the advancement of interregional trade in Caribbean live music. Lastly, the section on geographic proximity argues for earnest efforts to be made to implement the multi-destination tourism concept. It is envisaged that such efforts could ensure that the geographic closeness among Caribbean countries is harnessed for the purpose of increasing South-South and North-South interregional trade in Caribbean live music.

Notes

1 For more information on the North-South model see (Lewis 1954) "Economic Development with Unlimited Supplies of Labour." Also see (Goglio 1991) '"Technology Gap" theory of International Trade: A survey'.

An interesting read on the geography hypothesis on development between regions of the north and south is found in (Banerjee, Benahou and Mookherjee 2006).

2 See WTO website for more information https://www.wto.org/english/tratop_e/serv_e/gatsqa_e.htm.

References

Banerjee, Abhijit Vinayak, Roland Benabou, and Dilip Mookherjee. 2006. *Understanding Poverty*. New York: Oxford University Press.

Goglio, Alessandro. 1991. *"Technology Gap" Theory of International Trade: A Survey*. Vol. 22. Geneva: UNCTAD.

Lewis, Arthur. 1954. *Economic Development with Unlimited Supplies of Labour*. Vol. 22. 2 vols. Oxford: The Manchester School.

Savage, Mark. 2021. "Sir Elton John 'Livid' as BREXIT hits Musicians." *BBC News*, June 28.

Taglioni, Francois. 1997. "L'Association des Etats de la Caraibe dans les processus d'integration regionale." *Annales d'Amerique Latin et des Caraibes (HAL)* 14–15: 147–167.

UK Music. 2021. *This Is Music 2021*. London: UK Music.

World Trade Organization. 2022. *The General Agreement on Trade in Services (GATS): Objectives, Coverage and Disciplines*. Accessed August 27, 2022. https://www.wto.org/english/tratop_e/serv_e/gatsqa_e.htm.

2 The Economic Importance of Live Music Services

The Global Importance of Live Music Services

Through just observing the plethora of international live music festivals and expos, a few of which include, WOMEX, APAP, Global Fest, Atlantic Music Expo, and Visa for Music, it is easy to see why many might conclude that countries are deriving economic benefits from live music. After all, why would these festivals and expos, many of which offer technocratic sessions for networking and brainstorming, on ways to develop the world's music industries such as live music, continue to be annually held? Bearing this in mind, this chapter takes readers on a brief international tour to situate the economic significance of live music in areas such as the EU, the United Kingdom, East Asia (via South Korea), North America, and, finally, the Caribbean. Through this overview of the economic importance of festivals around the world, readers are expected to gain a clearer understanding as to why trade studies on live music services, such as the current one being proposed for live music services from the Caribbean, are important.

The Economic Importance of Live Music within the European Union

Europe, and specifically the EU, is among the regions of the world, which can be classified as an important global stomping ground for live music. The EU can be described as such, given that it is the home of the region's most popular music festivals such as Sziget in Hungary, Donauinselfest in Austria, Paleo in Switzerland, Exit in Serbia, and Pryzstanek Woodstock in Poland (L'hermite and Perrin 2014). These festivals attract scores of intraregional and extra-regional consumers. For the period 2012–2013, for example, attendance numbers for the above events ranged from 230,000–3.2 million patrons (L'hermite and

DOI: 10.4324/9781003343325-2

Perrin 2014). With such impressive attendance numbers at live music events within the EU, it is not surprising that within the sector of creative and cultural industries, live performance (inclusive of live music) is the category which accounts for over 1 in every 6 jobs in the EU (L'hermite and Perrin 2014). Moreover, the EU live music industry is a significant source of the region's revenue. In 2011, for instance, music festivals and other live music events on the continent generated a third of the total revenue for the region's live performance segment (L'hermite and Perrin 2014).

The Economic Importance of Live Music in the United Kingdom

In the United Kingdom (UK) live music also occupies a place of economic prominence. In terms of employment, live music supports the livelihoods of some 30,000 Brits (PricewaterhouseCoopers 2021). Live music's impact is so essential to the employment sector of this country, that when Brexit conditions made it harder for British live performers to trade their services in EU countries, British artistes like Sir Elton John sounded the alarm (Savage 2021). John raised concerns such as British emerging artistes no longer being able to benefit from visa-free travel, and the seeming sluggishness of UK policymakers to address the challenges concerning touring visa restrictions into the EU for emerging UK artists. Similarly, front-man Noel Gallagher of the British 90's band Oasis, like John, also underscored the importance of live music for employment in the United Kingdom when he expressed concerns about the reduction of employment opportunities for British artistes, since Brexit. Gallagher, for instance, described the negative impact of Brexit for British musicians who earn a living through live performance tours in the EU. Gallagher referenced that British musicians are presently forced to scale down the number of gigs in EU countries such as Germany and France because of the current exorbitant costs incurred to transport their equipment into these EU territories post Brexit (Savage 2021).

The Economic Importance of Live Music in South Korea

In South Korea, its entertainment services which include live K-pop (Korean Pop) music are given top priority within this country's economic agenda. The Korean, government, for example, grants subsidies to the country's private entertainment enterprises which manage and prepare live performing bands like BTS and Black Pink to export their services in both intraregional and extra-regional markets.[1]

The South Korean Government's subsidies to support this country's entertainment sector has reaped economic rewards for this East Asian country. It is reported, for example, that South Korea's export in its entertainment services has contributed to the development of the country's tourism. In 2014, for example, it was reported that South Korea's Pop music (K-pop) attracted over 12 million tourists into the country, a figure which represented a 12 percent uptick from the number of tourist arrivals in the previous year (Kim 2018). Moreover, the investments made by the South Korean government to support its country's private entertainment companies, have boosted the export of its live music services. It is reported that within the period commencing from the early 2000s to 2016, cultural exports such as K-pop music grew from 500 million USD to a whopping 6.3 billion in 2016 (Korea Creative Content Agency 2017 as cited in Kim 2018). Extra-regional markets where K-pop music is widely consumed include those of Europe and North America. In the United Kingdom, for example, it was reported that South Korea's most well-known K-pop band, BTS, on one occasion, sold out the entire Wembley Stadium in London, which has a holding capacity of 90,000 patrons (Lee 2020).

Economic Importance of Live Music in the United States

North America might be considered the global reference for observing the positive economic impact of live music. In the United States, for instance, the live music industry was reported to have generated a total nationwide revenue of $132.6 billion and accounted for 913,000 jobs in 2019 (Sacks and Mariano 2021). It was also reported that within that same year, visitor and capital expenditure for live music events amounted to $55.2 billion thanks to the spending of entertainment companies and concertgoers from out of town (Sacks and Mariano 2021). Furthermore, it was estimated that in 2019, this North American country's live music industry had brought in fiscal returns of $17.5 billion, which included federal tax revenues of approximately $9.3 billion and $8.3 billion in state and local tax returns (Sacks and Mariano 2021).

The Economic Importance of Live Music in the Caribbean

Within the Caribbean basin, the economic importance of cultural services and specifically that of live music is historically evident. Maurin and Watson (2019) allude to some of the oldest running music festivals such as the BVI Music Festival (British Virgin Islands), the Casals

Festival (Puerto Rico), the St Barts Music Festival (Saint Barthelemy), the Panorama Steelpan Festival (Trinidad and Tobago), and the Gwo-ka Festival (Guadeloupe), all of which underscore that governments within the region have observed the monetary value of live music within the Caribbean. This assumption relative to the financial importance of live music to the region appears to be supported by some of the data on Caribbean creative and cultural industries (CCIs). Maurin and Watson (2019), for example, sampled 202 live events from across 29 territories of the Caribbean and discovered that music-themed festivals accounted for the lion share at 41 percent. The Maurin and Watson (2019) study also illustrated that music-related events account for most festivals within the Caribbean basin. This should not come as a surprise since it has been argued that music events support the economies of island territories by attracting tourists to the region. This festival tourism has generated both employment and revenue within the region by way of providing income to the ancillary sectors of hotel and accommodation, air travel, ground transport, and food and beverage, to name a few. In the independent Anglophone Caribbean, the St Lucia Jazz Festival, Dominica's World Creole Music Festival, Barbados' Cropover Festival, Grenada's Spice Mas, Trinidad & Tobago's Carnival, and the Air Jamaica Blues and Jazz Festival are among some of the festivals based on live music in the region which make a compelling case for the positive economic impact of live music within the Caribbean basin.

The Economic Importance of Live Music in the Independent Anglophone Caribbean

The Economic Importance of Live Music for St Lucia

The *St Lucia Jazz Festival*, for instance, following a study conducted by (Nurse 2002), was said to have reaped returns of 7.0 million USD within a context where a capital of only 1.0 million USD had been injected towards staging this live music event. St Lucia's industry of hotel and accommodation is among the beneficiaries of the returns generated from the *St Lucia Jazz Festival*. It was reported that within the week of the St Lucia Jazz Festival, hotels around the island had an over 90 percent occupancy rate (Nurse 2002).

The Economic Importance of Live Music for Dominica

In Dominica, the importance of its live music industry is illustrated by the fact that it is an essential source of foreign exchange for the island. It was indicated that for countries like Dominica, the returns from festival tourism in 2005 ranged between 20 and 25 million USD (CARICOM 2006 as cited in Hendrickson et al. 2012). The monetary benefits derived from festivals within Dominica is perhaps best demonstrated by the State resources which are injected towards the annual staging of this island's flagship live music event, the *World Creole Music Festival* (WCMF), created in 1997. The event, which features French creole speaking artistes from across the globe, is known to attract a cadre of live music performers and tourists from the EU French Caribbean.

The Economic Importance of Live Music for Barbados

There is no doubt that Barbados has reaped financial rewards from its music industry, and its flagbearer Rihanna would have certainly contributed to the recognition of its live music industry on the world map. In terms of the economic importance of the island's live music services, the Crop Over festival serves as the reference. In 2012 then Prime Minister of Barbados, Freundel Stuart stated the importance of this festival to the Barbadian economy by citing that the total revenues generated from Crop Over in that same year amounted to $80 million, the currency was not specified (Holder 2012). In terms of the employment creation dividends produced by this festival, there are a number of stakeholders who are beneficiaries. These include stakeholders within the industries of tourism, transport, events management, and accommodation. Small and medium enterprises (SMEs) in security, food and beverage as well as hair and beauty, also earn income from this festival. It is noteworthy that post the COVID-19 pandemic, it appears that Barbados is strategising to promote South-South interregional trade in live music services between the Caribbean and Africa. On July 17, 2022, Nigerian, Grammy award winning, Afrobeats star Burna Boy performed live in Barbados for the first time at a live music event which was organised by local entertainment promoters and patronised by Barbadian Prime Minister Mia Motley. The event, in addition to Burna Boy, featured both local and regional acts from the Caribbean.

The Economic Importance of Live Music for Trinidad & Tobago

Trinidad & Tobago, like its Caribbean neighbours, has benefitted from forex returns from its festival economy. This Anglophone Caribbean, twin-island nation, arguably considered the festival epicentre of live music events within the region has approximately 3,000 artistes involved in live performance in a territory where over 200 live music events are recorded, most of which occur during the pre-Lenten Carnival season. Many of these events, particularly those related to Carnival, not only draw locals but also tourists from other islands and the diaspora communities in North America and the United Kingdom. These tourists spend within the range of 85USD–300USD just in entrance fees for these events and a whopping 1,000–2,000 USD per person to participate in the island-republic's street masquerades, so that they can dance for two days to the live music performed by the region's popular artistes (mode 2-consumption abroad).

Twenty years ago, when non-experimental studies were conducted on the economic importance of festivals in Trinidad & Tobago, it was reported that this country's Carnival annually attracted approximately 30,000 tourists which would contribute to visitor expenditures of 9.65 USD (Nurse 2002). However, currently experts have theorised that since then, visitor arrivals and visitor expenditures would have exponentially increased, with some hypothesising that current annual visitor arrivals to the country's Carnival are perhaps in the hundreds of thousands with average visitor expenditures of 5,000–8,000 USD within a 3–5 day period.

Based on these figures, experts have suggested that Caribbean diasporic visitors particularly those from Northern countries such as the United Kingdom are fuelling the income that this twin-island republic is generating from the festival of Carnival. Their assessment appears to hold merit given that export opportunities for live music services for Trinidadian artistes across cities in Germany, the United Kingdom, the United States, and Canada suggest that there is an extra-regional demand from the North for Caribbean live music services. Caribbean diaspora communities in the North have been credited for fuelling this demand and their apparent efforts have borne fruit. In the United Kingdom, for example, members of the Caribbean diaspora, after having modelled the Nottingham Carnival after Trinidad & Tobago's Carnival, have made this European festival a successful tourist attraction. The Nottinghill Carnival attracts swathes of interregional European visitors and to a lesser degree extra-regional Caribbean visitors who attend this event. Pre-Brexit, for example, the United Kingdom's Notting Hill Carnival in London was reported to have attracted 2 million visitors over two days (Nurse 2002). Given these kinds of numbers of visiting patrons, travelling to attend Caribbean-themed festivals in Europe and in North America, this would explain why some experts have noted annual opportunities for Caribbean musicians to do international tours. However, there are Caribbean economists who have expressed misgivings on how much of the monies earned from these international tours are re-invested in the Caribbean. Indeed, this is an issue which requires further empirical research, especially given that certain Caribbean economists have theorised that many of these Caribbean artistes who tour in Europe and North America either hold dual citizenship, residence status or have established overseas financial links which allow them to invest and save their earnings in the North rather than in the South. Hence, one can understand, why empirical studies on international trade in Caribbean live music services, exploring this issue, are of great import. There is also a need to take note of the fact that there is a growing degree of South-South intraregional trade in Caribbean live music services, as many of the region's independent Anglophone Caribbean live music patrons island-hop to attend the music festivals held in CARIFORUM countries throughout the year. This also provides the region's live music stakeholders with opportunities to trade their services regionally. However, again, like the data for North-South interregional trade, little is known as to how much profit gained from this form of South-South intraregional trade in Caribbean live music services is reinvested into the region, particularly in relation to the profits derived from touring (mode 4-movement of natural persons).

The Economic importance of Live Music for Non-Sovereign Caribbean Territories

Relative to non-sovereign Caribbean territories, such as those of the EU French Caribbean, studies on their festival economy are scarce. This is seemingly because of the EU French Caribbean philosophy on culture, which has been traditionally geared towards understanding the sociological benefits of culture to the populace rather than exploring its economic advantages.[2] Notwithstanding the lack of studies on the festival economy within the EU French Caribbean territories, available information suggests that in Guadeloupe, there is a booming local market for live music services. ONISEP (2015) reported, for instance, that in 2011 live music spawned 514 enterprises of the total 921 within the music industry of this EU French Caribbean territory. This suggests that live music services appear to be the most lucrative income generator for the island's music industry.[3] Live music services also account for the bulk of employment within Guadeloupe's music sector, accounting for 146 jobs out of the total of 257 within the music industry.

Guadeloupean economists Raboteur and Landais-Raboteur (2018) also conducted a study to arrive at a valuation of profits derived from the festival of Carnival in Guadeloupe. Raboteur and Landais-Raboteur (2018) selected as their case study, a French Caribbean Carnival pre-Lenten event known as the Dimanche Gras parade. Their study which was completed in 2012 revealed that during the Dimanche Gras parade, visitors contributed to average expenditures of 10.00 euros. The visitors who attended this event according to some experts represent North-South intraregional trade in Caribbean live music services, given that most of the patrons attending events in the EU French Caribbean territories hail from either mainland France or diaspora communities in neighbouring EU countries, in continental Europe (mode 2 consumption abroad). There is also inter-island consumption among the EU French Caribbean territories where respective populations visit each other's islands to attend live music events. This can also be classified as South-South intraregional trade.

Conclusion

In this chapter, one has been taken on a tour of the regions of East Asia, Europe, North America, and the Caribbean to observe the economic importance of live music. One has seen that live music is particularly important to economic issues which include job creation, tourism, and foreign exchange earnings. Therefore, it is certainly essential that emphasis is placed on experimental research to explore what are the factors which influence international trade in live music services globally.

Notes

1 Howard (2014) states that the South Korean government heavily supports entertainment companies in their efforts to export K-pop in intraregional and extra-regional markets.
2 A French economist informed the author that traditionally Guadeloupeans have not adopted an economic vision in the study of culture, thus explaining why most of the extant literature on culture within the French Antilles is not looked at from the perspective of trade but rather on non-economic topics such as cooperation.
3 See, ONISEP (2015: 20).

References

Hendrickson, Michael, Beverly Lugay, Esteban Perez Caldentey, Nanno Mulder, and Mariano Alvarez. 2012. *Creative Industries in the Caribbean: A New Road for Diversification and Export Growth*. Port of Spain: United Nations ECLAC (economic commission for Latin America and the Caribbean).

Holder, Sherie. 2012. "Crop Over a Major Revenue Earner." *Nation News Barbados*, November 11.

Howard, Keith. 2014. "Mapping K-Pop Past and Present: Shifting the Modes of Exchange." *Korea Observer* (ProQuest Central) 45 (3): 345.

Kim, Hun-Shik. 2018. *When Diplomacy Faces Trade Barriers and Diplomatic Frictions: The Case of the Korean Wave*. Vol. 14, in *Place Branding and Public Diplomacy*. Macmillan Publishers Ltd. https://doi.org/10.1057/s41254-017-0076-4

Lee, Alicia. 2020. *CNN Wire Service*, March.

L'hermite, Marc, and Bruno Perrin. 2014. *Les Secteurs culturels et creatifs europeens*. Paris: GESAC (Groupement europeen des societes d'auteurs et compositeurs).

Maurin, Alain, and Patrick K. Watson. 2019. "Unearthing and Analyzing Data on Festivals in the Caribbean." *Social and Economic Studies* (The University of the West Indies, Mona) 68 (1/2): 169–201. ISSN:0037-7651.

Nurse, Keith. 2002. "Bringing Culture into Tourism: Festival Tourism and Reggae Sunsplash in Jamaica." *Social and Economic Studies* (University of the West Indies, Mona) 51: 127–143.

ONISEP Guadeloupe. 2015. *Panorama Des Industries Culturelles et Creatives*. Les Abymes: ONISEP.

PricewaterhouseCoopers. 2021. *Perspectives from the Global and Media Outlook 2021–2025*. PricewaterhouseCoopers.

Raboteur, Joel, and Corrine Landais-Raboteur. 2018. *Essai d'apprehension de la valeur economique d'un evenement culturel majeur en Guadeloupe: le Carnaval. Esprit Critique*. https://www.esprit-critique.com/fiscalite/essai-dapprehension-de-la-valeur-economique-dun-evenement-culturel-majeur-en-guadeloupe-le-carnaval

Sacks, Adam, and Michael Mariano. 2021. *The Concerts and Live Entertainment Industy*. Oxford: Oxford Economics.

Savage, Mark. 2021. "Sir Elton John 'Livid' as BREXIT hits Musicians." *BBC News*, June 28.

3 Regionalism, International Trade Policy, and Caribbean Live Music Services

In mainstream global media, the Caribbean is often depicted as a homogenous expanse of sun, sea, and sand with little distinction in culture, politics, and economy. This presentation by the media can be forgiven, especially since there are many similarities among Caribbean territories. Notwithstanding these similarities, the Caribbean is equally a heterogenous region where islands differ in terms of their racial and ethnic demography, culture, economies, natural resources, and geopolitical frameworks. The geopolitical differences in the Caribbean are the result of a turbulent past of island conquests, by various European nations which imposed their own brand of culture and governance on the islands and peoples they subjugated. Many of these European powers, namely the Spanish, French, English, and Dutch enforced a system of colonial and post-colonial governance unique to the cultures and economic interests of their respective metropoles. Consequentially, varied geopolitical legacies introduced by these nations of the North remain in place today in the Caribbean. The French have kept control of the islands of Guadeloupe, Martinique, and St Martin and reconfigured them as overseas territories of France rather than colonies. The English relinquished their colonial ties to the independent English-speaking Caribbean societies by eventually ceding to their wishes of independence, but still, exercising a degree of geopolitical influence on them through the creation of the Commonwealth. The Dutch, like the French, reformulated their geopolitical relationship with their former new world colonies by designating them overseas territories of the Netherlands – the territories of St Maarten, Aruba, Curacao, and Bonaire are islands which remain geopolitically affiliated with Holland. And, there are some who strongly argue that the United States, newcomers to the region when compared to Europe, embarked upon their own brand of new-world conquest and colonialism by seizing protectorate-like control of Puerto Rico. The result of

DOI: 10.4324/9781003343325-3

these various incarnations of territorial conquest and relinquishment of power have now made the Caribbean, a geopolitically heterogenous zone which comes with its own complex issues for interregional trade in services such as live music.

The State of South-South and North-South Interregional Trade in Caribbean Live Music Services

The EU, including its overseas French Caribbean territories and the Anglophone CARIFORUM states, have been laying the groundwork for the development of trade in cultural services such as live music since 2010. Efforts made to develop this kind of trade between the two regional trading blocs are perhaps best illustrated by Guadeloupe (EU French Caribbean) and Trinidad & Tobago (Independent Anglophone CARIFORUM), as shall now be discussed.

In 2010, the first trade mission from Trinidad & Tobago to Guadeloupe which included representatives of the entertainment industry was funded by the grant assistance scheme programme from the European Commission's European Development Fund (EDF), a funding scheme which was made available following the signing of the EU-CARIFORUM Economic Partnership Agreement (EPA) in 2008. The agreement, signed by 15 CARIFORUM member States and 28 EU member countries, is aimed at facilitating bilateral activities in investment and trade between the two regional trading blocs (European Commission 2018). The Economic Partnership Agreement has within it, commitments which are of relevance for live music service providers from Anglophone CARIFORUM countries desirous of market entry into EU markets located in the Caribbean, such as Guadeloupe and in continental Europe, like Guadeloupe's metropole, France. This is because the commitments outlined in this agreement, in theory, bind EU countries to granting cultural service providers from CARIFORUM countries, entry into the EU region. However, even though the Economic Partnership Agreement is in theory a binding accord, the reality is that EU countries are under no obligation to permit entry to CARIFORUM service providers. The EU countries, having signed the Economic Partnership Agreement as individual states rather than as a bloc, can individually exercise discretion on whom they permit entry. Trade and economic experts from the English-speaking Caribbean have assessed that the right for EU member states to individually filter entry of CARIFORUM cultural service providers can be viewed as a non-tariff trade barrier. These experts have also referenced other conditions within the Economic Partnership Agreement that they have flagged as non-tariff barriers to trade. Some of the stipulations which have been deemed as trade barriers in this agreement are discussed in the following sections.

Formal Qualifications

The Economic Partnership Agreement specifies that entertainment service providers from the EU and CARIFORUM must furnish proof of their formal qualifications to be eligible for reciprocal market access through touring (mode 4). However, the reality is that many Caribbean live performers, though incredibly talented, are not formally trained either in the performing arts or in other non-related fields. Therefore, based on this condition within the agreement, this might automatically disqualify them from trading their services in North and South EU regions.

Visa Requirements

The current visa requirements within the Economic Partnership Agreement are non-binding, thus allowing each EU member state to apply visa restrictions and entry to CARICOM cultural practitioners as it sees fit, on a case-by-case basis. This could have deleterious consequences for Anglophone CARIFORUM emerging artistes who, because of not having the popularity and connections of more well-established CARIFORUM cultural service providers, might well miss out on opportunities to export their services into the French Caribbean EU because of these visa restrictions. These visa requirements are a significant obstacle to South-South interregional trade in live music services between sovereign and non-sovereign Caribbean territories. There are certain experts who have also concluded that visa requirements are the biggest obstacle to CARIFORUM artistes who wish to trade their music services within the continental EU. These experts have pointed out that the visa requirements could have the most deleterious impact on touring (mode 4), the primary mode through which live music stakeholders trade their live music services in the EU (Burri and Nurse 2019). Other trade experts have supported the theory that the visa requirements stipulated within the Economic Partnership agreement are an obstacle to trade in Caribbean live music services because they have observed that emerging artistes from the Caribbean are not sufficiently benefitting from the provisions within the agreement. They have noted that it is only the well-established live music service providers from the independent Anglophone CARIFORUM who are gaining increased touring opportunities within the EU (mode 4) (Chaitoo 2015).

Economic Needs Tests (ENTs)

With specific reference to the ENTs, these Caribbean experts have deemed them as non-tariff barriers to trade because it provides individual EU states a politically correct loophole to control who comes into their region, while avoiding the risk of being accused of violating the bilateral spirit of trade development within the agreement. ENTs are mechanisms used by countries to decide whether an employment service can be fulfilled locally or requires outsourcing abroad.

Limited Access to the Four Modes of Trade by Ancillary Live Music Stakeholders

The Economic Partnership Agreement might not be functioning as initially envisaged because during negotiations, considerations were not given to the importance of ancillary live music professionals for the development of interregional trade in Caribbean live music. The Economic Partnership Agreement (EPA) does not allow for the right of establishment of ancillary live music stakeholders such as producers, talent scouts, and promoters (mode 3).[1] This is because the EPA follows the CPC nomenclature that does not cover these kinds of live music services associated professions under mode 3 –right of establishment.[2] The Caribbean Regional Negotiating Machinery expert who negotiated with the European Commission argued that ancillary entertainment service providers were excluded from being covered in this agreement because the clear request from the English-speaking independent Caribbean was access for live entertainers in EU markets and that is reflected from the commitments made in the EPA for performers, not other ancillary services. The reasons given for why negotiators on behalf of the CARIFORUM entertainment sector did not give equal attention to trade in entertainment services via mode 3 (right of establishment) as they did to mode 4 (touring) were that they considered mode 3 (right of establishment) an impractical means of trade for CARIFORUM cultural stakeholders. It was argued that the high costs required to establish a company in the EU and the lack of contacts and intelligence within the EU that are needed for CARIFORUM ancillary live music service providers to be successful within EU markets would not have made mode 3 (right of establishment) a viable means of trade for CARIFORUM live music stakeholders.

Although it is understandable why members of the Caribbean Regional Negotiating Machinery would have channelled their energies towards negotiating for better conditions concerning touring in the EU (mode 4), it would have been equally worthwhile to also focus heavily on the other modes of trade such as commercial presence in the EU (mode 3) for ancillary professionals. After all, live music performers benefit from being supported by music producers, songwriters, entertainment management companies, radio stations, talent scouts, promoters, and even stylists and designers who all contribute to making live performers export-ready. Therefore, it is being argued that it would have been useful to live CARIFORUM performers, wishing to break into the EU markets of the North and South, to have been given the option to use support from EU ancillary service providers with offices in CARIFORUM countries.

In Trinidad & Tobago, for example, live performers have lamented on the lack of options they have in using EU entertainment management companies to make them export-ready for EU markets. Similarly, for EU live performers, they too would benefit from being able to use the services of independent Anglophone CARIFORUM live music professionals with a commercial presence in both North and South EU territories. These ancillary professionals given their knowledge of CARIFORUM tastes and networks within the CARIFORUM region and the diasporas in the North would have the skills to help EU live performers break into both intraregional and extra-regional CARIFORUM markets. There was even a case where an EU French Caribbean artiste, who in wanting to break into CARIFORUM markets, enlisted the assistance of a CARIFORUM producer to mix and master his music. The logic behind this decision taken by the EU French Caribbean live performer was to gain exposure in CARIFORUM markets because he reasoned that the CARIFORUM producer would have used his local media contacts to market his music to local listeners. Though a very proactive decision by the EU French Caribbean live music stakeholder, this turned out to be a very costly venture. He had to travel back and forth between his home country and that of the producer. It would have been so much easier for him if the CARIFORUM producer had the right to commercial presence in his home island.

Restrictions in Cross-Border Trade

The current policies of the Economic Partnership Agreement, particularly, relative to cross-border trade, have made trade in live music services between CARIFORUM and EU French Caribbean territories more arduous. Current cross-border trade policies implemented by the European Commission, through the agreement, restrict CARIFORUM live-streaming companies from trading their services within EU member states. This non-tariff trade barrier is unfortunate for CARIFORUM cultural service providers within an age where cultural products and services have become increasingly dematerialised because of innovations in information and communication technology (ICT), as shown by the pay-per-view livestream of music concerts, which were especially noticeable during the first two years of the COVID-19 pandemic. Even as we approach this post-pandemic period, we observe how cross-border trade is being used to amplify the consumption experience for consumers of live music services. The Swedish band ABBA, for instance, is making use of hologram technology for their worldwide tour. This technology permits the bandmembers to remain in Sweden while delivering their live performance before an audience in London, using younger hologram versions of themselves. Therefore, given the global importance of ICT for the development of cultural services trade, one sees the necessity for trade agreements that make provisions for cross-border exchange in services of this kind. However, the current CARIFORUM- EU Economic Partnership Agreement (EPA) makes no provisions for cross border exchange in cultural services like live music. Hence, one wonders if during the initial negotiations on the EPA between the European Commission and the Caribbean Regional Negotiating Machinery (CRNM), the CRNM considered how the exclusion of cross-border exchange on cultural services could negatively affect CARICOM's live music exports to Europe.[3]

The Low Volume of International Trade in Caribbean Live Music Services

The above issues deemed as trade barriers highlight the possible causes hampering the development of North-South and South-South interregional trade in Caribbean live music services. The fact that they have been theorised as trade barriers seems plausible given that findings from a recent (Gordon 2021) experimental study empirically showed that the volume of trade in South-South interregional trade in Caribbean live music services between the EU and the CARIFORUM is low.[4] Therefore, why are these issues not being adequately resolved with a sense of urgency? International trade and international relations experts, such as the late Norman Girvan (Jamaica) and Francois Taglioni (France), offer theories that might explain why this sense of urgency to address trade issues related to the development of international trade in Caribbean live music services is lost on institutional regional bodies of the North and the South. The theories of Girvan and Taglioni will be examined in the next section.

Regionalism: The Economic Partnership Agreement and Interregional Trade in Caribbean Live Music Services

There have been several arguments which give credence to the notion that the unfulfilled projects for Caribbean regional integration, the arguably biased free-trade arrangement such as the EU-CARIFORUM Economic Partnership Agreement, and the imbalance of power between regional trading blocs of the North and South have contributed to the lack of progress made in South-South and North-South interregional trade in Caribbean live music services. This section, therefore, will present these opinions.

Late Jamaican scholar in international relations and trade, Norman Girvan believes that the unfinished implementation of projects towards regional integration within the independent Anglophone Caribbean are to blame for why territories from this subregion have not been adequately equipped to take full advantage of their trade relationships with the EU through the Economic Partnership Agreement. Therefore, is it possible that the unfinished project of regional integration among Independent Caribbean states accounts for why both South-South trade and North-South interregional trade in Caribbean live music services are not adequately developed between the Anglophone CARIFORUM nations and the EU? Girvan's arguments seem to suggest this is the case. However before examining Girvan's arguments, it is important that readers are given a brief explanation of the CARICOM, the major regional institution within the English-speaking independent Caribbean.

The CARICOM (Caribbean Community)

CARICOM (the Caribbean Community) is a group of 20 Caribbean countries, 15 of which are permanent members comprising largely of independent Anglophone jurisdictions. These independent states within this regional trading bloc expand from the Bahamas in the Northern Caribbean to Belize in Central America and to Guyana in

South America. Relative to the trade and economic objectives of the CARICOM, they are as follows:

- the increase of opportunities for trade with extra-regional states;
- increased means of economic leverage and international competitiveness; and
- enhanced productivity (CARICOM n.d.).

CARICOM was founded in 1973 following a round of negotiations among regional leaders in Chaguaramas, Trinidad & Tobago. The resolutions arising from these negotiations would be later termed as The Treaty of Chaguaramas. However, in 2002, the treaty was revised to facilitate the creation of the Caribbean Single Market and Economy (CSME) – a project for realising CARICOM's trade and economic objectives for intraregional integration. It is the CSME, on which the next section will now focus. Arguments proffered on how the CSME project has failed in the development of intraregional trade will be analysed within the context of how this failure has impacted on South-South and North-South interregional trade in Caribbean live music services.

The Incomplete CSME Project and its Implications for Trade in Caribbean Live Music

Girvan (2009) alludes to some of the development issues within the Anglophone CARIFORUM states which might be impacting on their ability to trade in services with continental EU states and their overseas territories. He relates that the asynchronous implementation of key CSME policies within CARICOM member states has contributed to the region's failure to render its nations globally competitive within the framework of regional integration. He also laments that despite the noble project for facilitating regional integration among Caribbean states as stipulated within the Revised Treaty of Chaguaramas (1989), the project presently remains unachieved mainly because many individual CARICOM governments have not fully committed to implementing the economic recommendations enshrined in the project plan, within their local institutions.[5] There appears to be a great deal of merit to Girvan (2009)'s assertion on the asynchronous implementation of key international trade policies within the group of CARICOM countries (which make up the Anglophone CARIFORUM). This is because pertaining to the region's cultural industries (of which live music is a subset), one observes a disharmonised enactment of policies to increase the competitiveness of the region's cultural industries. This will be addressed in the next section.

Lack of CARICOM Unity during Negotiations with Powerful Northern Regional Trading Blocs

Hendrickson et al. (2012), for example, support Girvan (2009)'s assertion when they allude to the lack of team spirit within CARICOM when it comes to the promotion of the region's cultural industries. They observed that in the early 2000s, when CARICOM policymakers recognised the export potential of creative industries, initially strategies were centred around Barbados, Jamaica, and Trinidad and Tobago. The exclusion of the other CARICOM nations relative to these strategies suggests that there is a pervading lack of cohesion within this subregional economic bloc. Therefore, this lack of cohesion might have been the same approach that CARICOM representatives adopted during the 2004–2007 round of negotiations with the European Commission, aimed at defining, among other trade issues, the terms of trade for entertainment service providers within the Economic Partnership Agreement. Representatives of the Caribbean Regional Negotiating Machinery, who were assigned to conduct negotiations with the European Commission, on behalf of all 15 CARICOM countries, might have again, focussed on what the established live music stakeholders of Jamaica, Barbados and Trinidad & Tobago wanted, without an input from those who are cognizant of the needs of emerging artistes hailing from other CARICOM islands. The representatives of the Caribbean Regional Negotiating Machinery might have also overlooked during the negotiations, the considerations of the emerging artistes from Jamaica, Barbados, and Trinidad & Tobago. It is being argued, therefore, that the Economic Partnership Agreement, which in its present form, provides limited access to the 4 modes of trade in live music services, is the result of the habitual lack of strategic unanimity within the CARICOM especially during trade negotiations with Northern institutions. It is being recommended, therefore, that the problem of solidarity within the CARICOM during negotiations with Northern regional trading blocs, be seen as a matter of urgency. If not, South-South and North-South interregional trade in Caribbean live music services will continue to remain underdeveloped. Furthermore, failure in the CARICOM adopting a unified strategy with Northern regional institutions like the European Commission could result in individual Anglophone CARIFORUM countries seeing their interests steam-rolled by the EU, even if the EU trading partner is a Caribbean neighbour with which they share historical and cultural ties. This question of CARICOM disunity and the impact it could have on its negotiating leverage with the North shall be further analysed in the next section.

The Leverage of Regional Institutions of the North

It is an undisputed fact that individual small island states with small populations and economies cannot realistically achieve miraculous trade parity with an economic juggernaut like the European Union. Therefore, it is perplexing to observe how the governmental institutions of the Anglophone CARICOM do not seem to see the urgency in synchronously implementing programmes to ensure that the Caribbean Single Market and Economy (CSME) project is completed. At least, if completed, individual CARICOM states within the CARIFORUM, would be able to exert a degree of collective power, and consequently, have a fighting chance of exerting a minimum measure of real leverage during negotiations with the European Commission. Indeed, the proposed Caribbean Single Market and Economy held the promise of that leverage being a feasible prospect. However, today that project seems to be a mere figment of one's imagination. Since the project was first articulated in 1989, no common customs union has been formed nor has a single market nor common currency been realised within the Caribbean. Approximately 30 years after the CSME project was discussed in 1989, Caribbean economic disunity remains alive and well.

Indeed, this disunity among CARICOM states poses a real threat to the development of South-South and North-South interregional trade in Caribbean live music services. Therefore, Anglophone CARICOM states must urgently work towards establishing a unified thrust towards regionalism and an organised economic agenda. In so doing Anglophone CARIFORUM States will be in a position to assertively point out the disadvantages of the Economic Partnership Agreement for the region, and thus ensure that trade in Caribbean live music services is developed in a meaningful way. As it currently stands, regionalism among the Anglophone CARIFORUM countries continues to be weak and this is indeed lamentable within the current context of the Economic Partnership Agreement. Girvan (2009), for example, has sounded the alarm that the European Commission, through this agreement, is giving priority to the EU's global outreach economic agenda, at the expense of the economic interests of CARICOM. Girvan (2009) points out, for instance, that although the economic partnership agreements (EPAs) between Europe and several

African, Caribbean, Pacific (ACP) regions were, in principle, aimed at promoting sustainable development, addressing poverty, encouraging regional integration as well as supporting the international competitiveness of the ACP, in practice the Economic Partnership Agreement negotiations (2004–2007) revealed that the European Commission prioritised the regional interests of the EU over those of CARICOM. Girvan (2009) supports this assertion, by referencing the EPA negotiations (2004–2007) during which the Trade Directorate of the European Commission adopted a negotiating strategy whereby the framework of ACP economic partnership agreements gave priority to the EU's global trade policy objectives of expanding its export and investment opportunities in the developing South.[6] Girvan (2009) further substantiates his assessment about the European Commission's agenda with respect to the EPAs as being self-serving by referencing the fact that the European Commission fashioned its EPAs along the lines of the WTO framework, with the intention of using its leverage in legal and technical resources to benefit from the loopholes in current WTO rules.[7] Girvan (2009) supports his argument of the economic partnership agreements (EPAs) prioritising EU interests at the expense of the ACP by alluding to the European Commission having implemented within these agreements, policies of investment, competition and government procurement into the framework of the EPA negotiations, proposals which he states were the "so called Singapore issues which were rejected for inclusion in the Doha Round at the 6th WTO Ministerial Conference in Cancun 2003". It would appear that by making reference to the fact that the European Commission incorporated within the EPA framework these rejected proposals, the Jamaican international relations specialist is making the claim that this EU body purposefully implemented within the EPAs, these rejected Singapore issues, in order to take full advantage of the market liberalisation opportunities that these proposals would have afforded them within ACP countries with weaker legal and technical resources.

In relation to cultural industries, of which live music is a subset, CARICOM academics specialising in cultural issues seem to provide more context to the (Girvan 2009) assertion of the Economic Partnership Agreement being essentially a self-interested mechanism for the EU's international trade agenda. There are specific contemporary CARICOM scholars, who support the analysis of (Girvan 2009), by providing their critique on the Protocol on Cultural Cooperation within the EPA. However, before referencing their analysis on the Protocol for Cultural Cooperation, it is important to understand its intended purpose. The Protocol for Cultural Cooperation provides recommendations for non-commercial projects and programmes to facilitate trade in cultural services. It is considered that emerging entertainers who have never traded their services in the EU stand to benefit the most from this protocol (Chaitoo 2013).[8] The Protocol on Cultural Cooperation is viewed as such, because it is believed that emerging CARIFORUM artistes would be able to enter EU countries for non-commercial purposes like training and not-for-profit concerts, that could eventually lead to them securing trading opportunities within the EU. The protocol therefore is seen as a mechanism for increasing exposure and building professional networks that could overtime lead to emerging artistes securing business opportunities within the EU (Chaitoo 2013).

Although, the provisions within this Protocol an Cultural Cooperation look optimistic for boosting trade in cultural services between the EU and CARIFORUM, Caribbean scholars in culture have flagged this protocol. They believe that the conditions in the protocol are disadvantageous for Caribbean creatives who wish to monetise their works in EU Countries. In order to support this point, they allude to article 5 of the protocol which stipulates that co-produced EU-CARIFORUM audio-visual content can only be considered eligible for sale in EU countries such as France, provided that 80 percent of the production is done in the EU and 20 percent done in a CARIFORUM territory. They bemoaned this stipulation within the protocol because they considered that it prevented CARIFORUM countries from attaining an equal degree of market access for distribution and retail of cultural services that would be accorded to EU countries. For these Caribbean scholars, the idea that the Economic Partnership Agreement market access provisions are disproportionately skewed in favour of the EU, is supported by the fact that CARIFORUM cultural practitioners might not benefit from borderless market access to the extent that EU countries could. Indeed, many scholars agree that given that CARIFORUM countries signed on as a regional trading bloc whereas the EU signed on as individual countries, makes borderless market access more of a reality for the EU than it is for the CARIFORUM.

Indeed, Girvan (2009)'s assessment appears to resonate within certain quarters of the CARICOM intelligentsia who like Girvan appear to agree that the Economic Partnership Agreement is a biased agreement privileging the globalisation agenda of the EU over those of the CARICOM/ Anglophone CARIFORUM. They have described the regionalism model of the Economic Partnership Agreement as "one of asymmetrical, neo-colonial and neo-liberal integration between a large highly developed centre economy and a set of small disconnected peripheral economies of varying levels of development (Brewster 2008 as cited in Girvan 2009)." Therefore, one must ask if the disunited structure of CARICOM countries is what might have negatively affected their representatives' ability to negotiate for better terms within the Economic Partnership Agreement with respect to trade in entertainment services like live music. It is possible.

Much has been discussed in the above sections, on how the lack of cohesiveness within CARICOM, as well as the tendency of the EU to privilege its economic priorities overs those of the CARICOM, could be the fundamental causes of the issues which plague both North-South and South-South interregional trade in Caribbean live music services between the two regions. However, it is also important to assess how non-sovereign Caribbean territories as well as their relationships with their European metropoles have contributed to these interregional trade problems. This will be explored in the next section.

The Role Played by Non-Sovereign States in the Development of Interregional Trade in Caribbean Live Music Services

Caribbean scholars, as seen in the previous sections, attribute the underdevelopment in interregional trade in Caribbean services to the lack of cohesion among independent Anglophone Caribbean countries. They also attribute the unsatisfactory progress made in interregional trade in Caribbean services to what they note as the EU's agenda of economic expansion in the South under the pretext of championing reciprocal market access through the Economic Partnership Agreement. However, little has been written on the role that non-sovereign EU Caribbean territories have played in the lack of development in interregional trade in Caribbean services. Furthermore, enough has not been said about how their relationship with their European metropoles has factored into the lack of progress made in trade in Caribbean services, like live music. This section therefore examines these issues by referencing the case of the EU French Caribbean territories, and their relationship with France and the EU.

The Lack of Cohesion among Non-Sovereign EU Caribbean Territories

The non-sovereign EU Caribbean territories, particularly the overseas French territories, do not seem to move as a united front when it comes to negotiating for improved conditions of trade in services with their independent Anglophone neighbours. Their past efforts to strengthen their economic relationships with their CARIFORUM neighbours appear to be unilateral in a nature, with each territory wishing to protect their own autonomy, despite being under the geo-political jurisdiction of France and the EU. The assumption that a fraternal spirit among the EU French Caribbean territories is lacking can be supported by the different periods the islands of Guadeloupe and Martinique attained associate membership in the Organisation of Eastern Caribbean States (OECS). Martinique became a member in 2016 after making a formal request for entry into this regional bloc, largely comprised of independent Caribbean states. Guadeloupe, on the other hand, only became a member of the OECS three years after Martinique, in 2019. It is therefore being argued that the different periods in membership accession into the OECS between Martinique and Guadeloupe are perhaps an indication that their respective trade policy agendas with the CARIFORUM are not conceptualised in a united manner. If indeed, there is truth to this theory, this might be among the causes of why South-South interregional trade in their live music services with the Anglophone CARIFORUM is lacking. Therefore, it is being suggested that empirical research be conducted to examine what might be the source of this possible disunity among overseas EU Caribbean territories. Research of this nature is truly needed at this time. The findings from such a study might provide the basis upon which overseas EU Caribbean territories can collec-tively strategise for increased leverage in their negotiations with their European metropoles and thus allow them to jointly advocate for increased autonomy to re-imagine the kind of interregional trade relationship they would wish to have with their independent Anglo-phone CARIFORUM peers.

However, apart from the argument that disunity among non-sovereign states might account for why they have not been able to advance the development of trading their live music with their Anglophone CARI-FORUM neighbours, there might be other reasons at play. Discussion on these reasons will be reviewed in the following section.

The Non-independent EU Territories' Relationships with their European Metropoles: How They Affect Trade in Caribbean Live Music Services

It is certainly important to explore how the relationship that non-independent EU territories have with their European metropoles affects international trade in Caribbean services like live music. In the case of the Overseas Caribbean territories of France it is worthwhile to reflect on the following:

- Are these territories beholden to mainland France to act as proxies for EU economic interests within the Caribbean region?
- Are they granted sufficient autonomy within the EPA framework to determine the kind of cultural services trade relationship they would wish to entertain with their independent Anglophone neighbours?
- With respect to cultural services trade like that of live music, what role, if any, has the difference in these territories' language (French) played in relation to their English-speaking neighbours who make up the majority of the Caribbean region?

These, as well as other important questions will be discussed for further contextualisation of the part played by the non-independent EU Caribbean territories, in what seems to be a lack of development in their trade in cultural services with the independent Anglophone CARIFORUM countries, despite the Economic Partnership Agreement. Perhaps, the following anecdote would provide further contextualisation of the challenges experienced by the EU French Caribbean territories which might account for why there is a seeming lack of development of their cultural services trade with the Anglophone CARIFORUM States.

The late Guadeloupean/French music icon, Jacob Desvarieux, was interviewed by this author, just before his group's appearance (Kassav') at the CARIFESTA closing concert in Trinidad and Tobago, July 2019. During the interview, it was surprising to learn from Desvarieux, that Caribbean fans, who awaited with bated breath to see Kassav' perform that night, might have nearly missed this opportunity. Desvarieux revealed during the interview, that he and his band members were almost forbidden from performing that night by the French Government because of a wrangling which arose between the French State and the Regional Council of Guadeloupe (The governing body charged with managing the interests within the island). The conflict arose from the fact that mainland France was insisting that Kassav' should perform under the banner of France whereas, the Guadeloupean Regional Council was adamant that Kassav' should represent the island of its origin, Guadeloupe. In the end, it was agreed by both parties that Kassav' would be presented as hailing from the island of Guadeloupe. This anecdote serves to present the conundrum within which the French territories of the Americas find themselves concerning their relationship between their metropole and their sovereign Caribbean neighbours. Therefore, it is reasonable to surmise that the dilemma of the French Caribbean EU territories of managing their geopolitical affiliation with France while striving for a more meaningful regional relationship with their independent neighbours might be an obstacle to their trading in live music services with Anglophone CARIFORUM countries.

French scholar, Francois Taglioni explores the difficulties experienced by the French Caribbean EU territories in strengthening their economic relationships with their independent Anglophone neighbours within a paper he published in 1997. Taglioni (1997) assesses that although the French overseas departments of the Americas have for several years made attempts to forge partnerships of all forms with their sovereign Caribbean neighbours, they remain marginalised. He attributes their marginalisation to a deliberate attempt by mainland France to divide them from their independent regional neighbours. In order to develop this point, Taglioni (1997) makes reference to a system of 'self-sub-regionalism' among these territories; a kind of regionalism which has required the overseas French Caribbean territories to amalgamate themselves as one region and assimilate with Metropolitan France. This system of amalgamation and assimilation has been in existence since 1946.

It would appear that this system of marginalisation imposed on the French Caribbean EU territories to separate them from the rest of the independent Anglophone Caribbean remains in place today. In a recent parliamentary report published in 2020 presenting a strategic framework for diplomatic engagement for the French overseas departments of the Americas with their sovereign neighbours, the authors of this report (Chapelier and Peletti 2020) describe the regionalism initiatives between the EU French Caribbean territories and their independent neighbours as "embryonic". Therefore, this begs the question: why has this marginalisation persisted despite the French Caribbean EU territories' overtures to establish economic relationships with their neighbours for over decades? The answer may lie, once again, with the Girvan (2009) theory of the EU privileging their economic interests within the region, even at the expense, it would appear, of those of their overseas territories within the Caribbean. This assessment appears clearly borne out in the Chapelier and Peletti (2020) report. The authors of this report, in proposing a diplomatic strategy for the EU French Caribbean territories with their independent Anglophone neighbours, formulate this strategy around three principles; two of which require that France uses its overseas territories to "strengthen its influence in the world" and to "allow for Europe's expansion in the world (Chapelier and Peletti 2020)." Only one out of the three principles behind this strategy of regionalism refers to the actual benefit for overseas French Caribbean departments – that benefit being to offer these territories "a level of development which is equal to that of their (Anglophone CARIFORUM) neighbours and an opportunity to affirm the identity they have in common with their regional neighbours[9]."

Indeed, having to operate within a diplomatic framework where the EU dictates how these overseas French Caribbean territories ought to relate with their Anglophone sovereign peers creates a dichotomous situation for territories like Guadeloupe in its cultural services trading relationship with Trinidad & Tobago. The dichotomy is that Guadeloupeans might be aware and empathise with their Anglophone CARIFORUM neighbours who face obstacles to trade in cultural services within EU territories such as Guadeloupe, however, they are virtually powerless in assisting their regional partners given that their geopolitical agenda is prescribed by parliamentarians in mainland France and the European Commission.

The Association of Caribbean States (ACS), one would have hoped, might have been able to be an effective mediator in negotiations around these issues. After all, the ACS has the mandate of bringing together states and territories of the Caribbean basin, irrespective of their geopolitical and economic affiliations so that it can act as a facilitator to its 39 member countries relative to initiatives on areas such as culture, ICT, and trade (Fabry 2005). However, as Fabry (2005) points out, the ambitious mandate of the ACS far exceeds the budget allocated to the association to carry out its mission as regional facilitator. Hence, this might also account for why, despite the Economic Partnership Agreement, it seems that trade in live music services between CARIFORUM States and the French Caribbean EU territories such as Guadeloupe, have not progressed as had been initially envisaged over ten years ago.

However, it is certainly erroneous to transfer the bulk of the responsibility of facilitating South-South interregional trade in live music services to the Caribbean to the ACS. Responsibility should also lie with Caribbean leadership to address the language gap issue, as shall be discussed in the following section.

The Language Difference Bogeyman and Other Impediments to South-South Interregional Trade in Caribbean Live Music Services

The language difference issue is arguably an aspect which Caribbean leadership sweeps under the carpet. Yet, the reality is that it is a hurdle that must be overcome if interregional services trade of any kind is to flourish. In the case of the Caribbean, scholars such as French academic Francois Taglioni have contemplated on the language gap problem and its economic implications for interregional trade within the Caribbean. Taglioni (1997) concludes that the greatest of all impediments to South-South interregional integration in the Caribbean is the reciprocal lack of knowledge of the other's language. In the case of the overseas French territories of the Americas, he attributes their lack of proficiency in English to their dependency "reflex" to turn to mainland France to supply their needs; a reflex, which, as he concludes, has been conditioned by Metropolitan France, for centuries.

Taglioni (1997)'s assessment on the fact that the lack of reciprocal knowledge of the other's language is a serious obstacle to economic regionalism between EU French Caribbean territories and Anglophone CARIFORUM islands is evident in the trade of cultural services between the two regions. CARICOM academics in culture, for example, allude to the fact that Anglophone CARIFORUM cultural stakeholders, in order to secure funding from the EU for their projects, are encouraged to complete very time consuming and lengthy request forms in the language of the EU country from which the funding is being sourced. They opined that this procedure was unfair to emerging artistes from the Anglophone CARIFORUM countries who (unlike the popular artistes of the region) might not have the foreign language skills nor financial resources to employ the services of a translator/interpreter.

Hence, bearing in mind the above observations of Taglioni (1997) and other CARICOM scholars, there is an immediate need for a series of empirical studies to be conducted on the role that language differences play in international trade not only within the music industry of the Caribbean but also for other services industries which might not be necessarily cultural in nature. Furthermore, apart from language, the role of other factors ought to be given consideration. These should include non-tariff barriers such as visa restrictions, economic needs tests, quotas in consumption of foreign cultural imports, cross-border trade restrictions, differences in foreign policy agenda, intellectual property ownership conditions, differences in rates of exchange in currency, transport as well as the size and influence of the regional trading blocs to which a given Caribbean territory belongs. Results from this kind of experimental research could provide the requisite data for policymakers to conceptualise strategies on regionalism that might have the desirable impact on advancing services trade between the independent and non-independent territories of the Caribbean, inclusive of that of live music.

Conclusion

Non-tariff trade barriers, disunity within Anglophone independent states, the tendency for Europe to champion its economic interests at the expense of the Caribbean, the lack of solidarity among non-sovereign Caribbean territories, and the difficult geopolitical relationships these non-sovereign Caribbean territories have with their metropoles of the North have all been addressed in this chapter. This chapter, through referencing where necessary, the theories of Caribbean and European interested parties on these matters, has hopefully achieved its goal. The goal of awakening the curiosity of international readers to pursue empirical studies on factors impacting North-South and South-South trade in Caribbean live music services. The next chapter, therefore, proposes an easy-to follow approach which can be applied to experimental research on this trade.

Notes

1 Author received confirmation of this information by a former Caribbean Regional Negotiating Machinery expert (CRNM).
2 This was confirmed by one of the CRNM operatives who was heavily involved in the negotiations between the EU and the CARIFORUM prior to the signing of the EPA in 2008. More details on this are found in Gordon (2021).
3 The question on whether the CRNM was fully cognizant of the negative implications for Caribbean cultural service providers due to the exclusion of cross-border exchange provisions within the Economic Partnership Agreement is valid, particularly now, as CARICOM companies are making use of technology to increase international trade. In August 2022, for example, a Trinidadian telecommunications company launched an e-vending platform so that Caribbean artisans would be able to upload images of their handcrafted items and attract potential consumers within the region and diaspora markets in the North.
4 Author's dissertation empirically confirmed that the EU-CARIFORUM Economic Partnership Agreement was not having a significant impact in developing South-South interregional trade in Caribbean live music services. The results from that study showed that the volume of trade currently remains very low. The mean value for the volume of trade in live music services between the EU French Caribbean and Anglophone CARIFORUM following regression analysis was 1.86, a mean score well below the alpha 5. The mean value showing the low volume of trade was based on the subset of 5 questions extracted from exploratory factor analysis and then used in regression to measure trade volumes in live music services between the two subregions. Those 5 questions were relied upon for measuring the volume of trade because scientific statistical modelling techniques indicated that they generated the most consistent responses from Caribbean live music stakeholders who were surveyed on the question of trade volume in live music.

5 Girvan (2009) laments that despite the "the legal framework of the CSME as enshrined within the Revised Treaty of Chaguaramas (1989)" for facilitating " Open Regionalism," among CARICOM states, "specific implementation measures have been left to the discretion of CARICOM organs of governance," which operate under the purview of the governments of the individual CARICOM member states they represent (Girvan 2009).

6 Girvan (2009) supports his claim of the European commission using the EPA for the benefit of the EU's trade agenda at the expense of the CARICOM when he states that the "the European Commission's Trade Directorate adopted a negotiating strategy that cast EPAs within the framework of the EU's global trade policy objectives aimed at opening markets in emerging economies to European exporters and investors."

7 Girvan (2009) makes the claim that the European Commission fashioned its EPAs along the lines of the WTO framework, with the intention of using its leverage in legal and technical resources "to exploit ambiguities in existing WTO rules."

8 Chaitoo (2013) states that the "the protocol mechanism is particularly useful for the less well-established artists, entertainers and other cultural practitioners who are not operating commercially in the EU."

9 Author's translation of original (Chapelier and Peletti 2020) report in French.

References

Burri, Mirra, and Keith Nurse. 2019. *Culture in the CARIFORUM-European Union Economic Partnership Agreement: Rebalancing Trade Flows between Europe and the Caribbean?* Paris: UNESCO (United Nations Educational and Scientific and Cultural Organization).

CARICOM. n.d. "Who We Are." *CARICOM Caribbean Community.* Accessed November 10, 2022. https://caricom.org/our-community/who-we-are/.

Chaitoo, Ramesh. 2013. *The Entertainment Sector in CARICOM.* IDB Inter-American Development Bank.

———. 2015. "The Music Sector and CARIFORUM-EU Trade Relations." *The Third Cariforum EU Business Forum.* Port of Spain: Caribbean Export Development, 1–12.

Chapelier, Annie, and Berangere Peletti. 2020. *Rapport d'information sur l'environnement international des departements et collectivites d'outre-mer.* Parliamentary Report, Paris: Assemblee Nationale.

Fabry, Veronique. 2005. "L'Outre mer dans les ensembles regionaux." *Pouvoirs: Revue d'etudes constitutionnellles et Politiques* (CAIRN) 113: 137–151. ISSN: 2101–0390.

Girvan, Norman. 2009. "Implications of the Economic Partnership Agreement (EPA) for the CSME." *Social and Economic Studies* (Routledge) 58 (2): 91–127.

Gordon, Lisa. 2021 (Submitted). *Doctoral Thesis: The Trade in Live Music Services between European Union French Caribbean Territories and Anglophone CARIFORUM Countries: The Case Study of Guadeloupe and Trinidad & Tobago.* St Augustine: The University of the West Indies, St Augustine Campus.

Hendrickson, Michael, Beverly Lugay, Esteban Perez Caldentey, Nanno Mulder, and Mariano Alvarez. 2012. *Creative Industries in the Caribbean: A New Road for Diversification and Export Growth.* Port of Spain: United Nations ECLAC (economic commission for Latin America and the Caribbean).

Taglioni, Francois. 1997. "L'Association des Etats de la Caraibe dans les processus d'integration regionale." *Annales d'Amerique Latine et des Caraibes* (HAL) 14–15: 147–167.

4 Introduction to Experimental Studies on International Trade and the Music Industry

Complex algorithms and analytics integrated within entertainment streaming platforms illustrate how the world is fast becoming more data driven. Job advertisements within entertainment industries which call for candidates' knowledge on computing statistical modelling tools such as R, SPSS, or STATA indicate that empirical data is being sought after for the study of entertainment services. Despite these global trends towards empirical data, in the Caribbean, experimental studies on trade in cultural services, like live music are lacking. There may be several reasons why this is the case. A key reason is the challenge of data availability in the Caribbean. It is very difficult to apply complex econometrical techniques of analysis when the requisite data is either non-existent or of a poor quality. Maurin and Watson (2002), for example, have alluded to the questionable quality of data in the Caribbean, citing issues such as datasets with missing values or lacking in uniformity. They attribute these issues to several factors, some of which include the inconsistent and infrequent fashion in which Caribbean data are collected.

Another issue which might be affecting the shortage of data on trade in Caribbean cultural services, such as live music, is the difficulty in accessing information on the earnings of live music stakeholders. Caribbean live music stakeholders are often reluctant to disclose their earnings for confidentiality reasons. Furthermore, national tax collection institutions, which have this information, often do not share it with the public. Taking note of these issues of data access and data quality on international trade in Caribbean entertainment services, this chapter presents an approach to deal with them. The proposed approach, which is not dependent on sourcing the earnings of Caribbean live music stakeholders, requires merging international trade theory with statistical modelling techniques. This approach was used in the Gordon (2021) study which empirically measured the volume of

DOI: 10.4324/9781003343325-4

South-South interregional trade in Caribbean live music services. The research design was also useful for identifying what were the factors impacting on this trade.

Among the advantages of the proposed research approach is its structured sequence of five steps. These five steps will be explained in the next section. The five-step feature of this research design makes it easy to be understood and to be replicated by researchers of all levels of experience. Through the replicated use of this proposed research design, it is envisaged that with the effluxion of time, more coherent and reliable datasets will be produced. These reliable datasets will no doubt assist the region's governing bodies, in making effective evidence-based policies, to support the development of international trade in Caribbean live music services. They might also help econometricians in their macroeconomic studies of Caribbean cultural industries. The next section briefly explains the proposed approach.

An Easy to Follow Five-Step Approach for Studies on Live Music Services in the Caribbean

These simple five steps will introduce readers to the ABCs of conducting an experimental study on international trade in Caribbean live music services. The approach was initially used in the Gordon (2021) study on trade in live music services between the EU French Caribbean territories and Anglophone CARIFORUM countries (South-South interregional trade) but it can also be applied to North-South interregional trade (Caribbean and the continental EU) as well as North-South intraregional trade (the continental EU and its overseas Caribbean territories).

Summary of Research Design

This section summarises each of the five steps of the empirical methodology as seen in the illustration above. These steps are as follows:

1 Step One: This is the compass which guides this study. Here the Linder hypothesis of international trade is the chosen conceptual framework, and both the variables and hypotheses are defined (The Linder hypothesis will be briefly described in the next section).

2 Step Two: This is the data collection phase. It is being recommended that a minimum of 150 live music stakeholders be recruited to source primary data on at least seven variables. The instrument

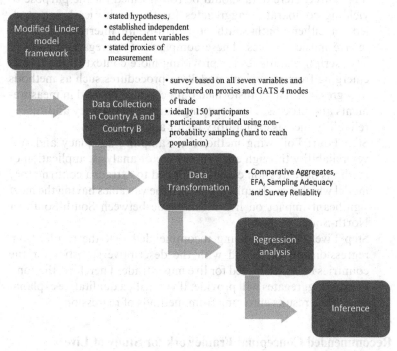

Figure 4.1 A five-step approach for experimental studies on live music trade

to be used should be a survey administered in the native languages of the countries or regions being studied. The survey should be structured on the variables chosen for the study and the four modes of trade as stipulated in the General Accord of Trade in Services (GATS) of the WTO (The World Trade Organisation). A Likert-like scale of 1–5 should be integrated into the survey. This will allow participants to register how much they agree or disagree with a statement seeking to find out how a variable is impacting on trade in live music between, for example, a French Caribbean overseas territory like Guadeloupe and an independent Anglophone CARIFORUM territory such as Trinidad &Tobago. "1" on the scale could represent strongly disagree and thus permit participants to indicate how much they feel a variable is having a negative impact on live music services trade, whereas "5" on the scale can represent (strongly agree), therefore allowing participants to show how they believe a variable is having a positive impact on this trade. "3" should represent the midpoint/average.

3 Step Three: Here data should be transformed for the purpose of yielding comparative aggregates for the territories being studied for either South-South or North-South interregional trade in live music services. These comparative aggregates can serve as descriptive statistics for providing more context to the results emerging from statistical modelling procedures such as methods of regression. The transformed data can also be used in measurements and processes for verifying sampling adequacy and survey reliability such as exploratory factor analysis (EFA).

4 Step Four: Following methods of sampling adequacy and survey reliability through exploratory factor analysis, application of methods of regression could be applied to extract a confirmatory model which would explain what are the variables having the most significant impact on live music trade between South-South or North-South regions.

5 Step Five: Here it is being recommended that the results from regression are compared with the descriptive statistics for the countries being examined for live music trade. Therefore, the comparative aggregates will provide, if you will, a qualitative explanation of the results emerging from methods of regression.

Recommended Conceptual Framework for Study of Live Music Trade

Within the five-step approach, the conceptual framework constitutes the first step. It is being recommended that for studies on South-South of North-South interregional/intraregional trade in cultural services like live music, that the Linder hypothesis be adopted as the conceptual framework. This Linder model of international trade theory seems most applicable to studies on trade in cultural services like live music because, it is a theory specifically conceptualised for interregional trade between similar territories. It also allows for multiple variables to be studied, which is crucial for studies on cultural services industries like live music. This is because, cultural services, unlike traditional, non-cultural industries, are heavily influenced by cultural considerations such as colonial heritage, language, and musical tastes. Cultural services can also be greatly influenced by sociological issues like racism. French Caribbean live music stakeholders, for example, have considered whether the problems they face in being employed for gigs in metropolitan France stems from racism.[1] Therefore, a theoretical framework which allows for the inclusion of race and ethnicity as variables is highly important for a study on live music trade. The basic premise of the Linder hypothesis is that the more two countries are similar the more they trade. Like traditional international trade models, the Linder hypothesis was originally conceptualised for trade in goods but is now applied for the study in services trade. The image below is a visual representation of the theoretical framework based on the Linder hypothesis, which was used in the Gordon (2021) study, examining trade in live music services between the EU French Caribbean territory, Guadeloupe, and the Anglophone CARIFORUM country, Trinidad & Tobago.

One is under no obligation to follow this proposed theoretical framework to the letter. It is expected that the selection of variables will vary based on individual research contexts. However, it is being strongly advised that when using this theoretical framework, the variables of demand and volume of trade be included. This is because when (Linder 1961) conceptualised his hypothesis, he stressed the importance of exploring the relationship between consumer demand and volume of trade.

Within the diagram below the principal hypothesis is based on the basic premise of the Linder model: The more two countries are similar the more they trade. The secondary hypotheses are based on the six independent variables which were chosen for the Gordon (2021) study on interregional trade in Caribbean live music services. In this visual representation it is hypothesised that similarities in consumer demand, technology, trade facilitation measures, culture, legal institutions, and geographic proximity affect the volume of trade in live music services.

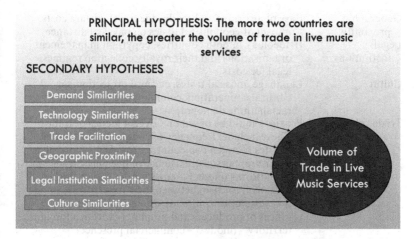

Figure 4.2 Visual representation of proposed theoretical framework for studies on interregional trade in live music services

Once the variables have been selected, it is important to attach proxies to them. Proxies are measurable units which are associated with a
variable. In the case of live music trade, proxies would help us determine the volume of trade and the independent variables having either a
positive or negative impact on this trade. The matrix below is an illustration of possible variables and their proxies which could be applied
to experimental studies on live music trade. However, readers should
feel under no obligation to follow this selection of variables because
only you can determine, based on your context of study on interregional trade in entertainment services, which variables are the most
pertinent. However, it is strongly advised that two variables always be
included in your study if you plan on using this proposed approach.
These are demand and volume of trade. This is because Linder (1961)
deemed exploring the relationship between those variables as being
crucial when applying his country similarity model (Table 4.1).

Table 4.1 Recommended variables and their proxies

Variable	Proxies
Demand	per capita income, market size, saving habits, consumer spending habits for entertainment services
Technology	High-speed internet infrastructure, consumption practices on digital platforms, marketing campaigns on digital platforms, usage of technology by local cultural service providers for cross-border trade
Trade facilitation	Artist registries, immigration laws, bilateral trade events
Geographic proximity	Ease of airbridge and sea-bridge travel, airfare costs, impact of geopolitical issues on physical distance
Legal institutions	IP ideology in both countries, copyright management organisations and their royalty collection regimes, legal fee costs
Culture	Language, musical tastes, cultural protectionism, cultural cooperation, colonial history, religion, racial/ethnic demography
Trade volume	Proxies should be based on GATS 4 modes of trade. These include: frequency of concert tours from artistes between two countries (mode 4 – movement of natural persons), existence of live music trade via E-platforms (mode 1 – cross border trade), frequency of festival tourism between the two territories (mode 2 – consumption abroad), existence of studios and offices of producers and promoters within a foreign territory – (mode 3 – commercial presence)

Statistical Modelling Methods

Upon the completion of surveys based on chosen variables and the GATS four modes of trade, statistical modelling methods can be used for two purposes: to test for sampling adequacy and survey reliability, and to determine which of the variables have a significantly positive or negative impact on live music services interregional/intraregional trade. Exploratory factor analysis (EFA), for example, is often used to test for sampling adequacy and survey reliability. Methods of regression are used for testing the significance and the impact of the independent variables on live music trade. There are several texts which provide detailed information on the use of these techniques.[2]

Sampling and Data Transformation

When conducting surveys, it is important to select a sample from a population of cultural practitioners (such as those in live music), representing the countries which are being studied. If, for example, research is being conducted on interregional live music trade between non-independent and independent territories in the Caribbean, it would be important to draw a sample from a population of live music stakeholders from both regions. When considering live music stakeholders, the first thing that might come to mind is just the performers, but one must also consider the ancillary live music professionals who support and benefit from this trade. They include the talent scouts, promoters, managers, disc-jockeys, music producers, and entrepreneurs of livestreaming platforms.

The conventional theory is that experimental studies require probability sampling methods. However, in the case of recruiting live music stakeholders, this technique might not be practical. This is because live music professionals can be a hard-to-reach population based on their very busy schedules. They are often on tour or have studio commitments. Moreover, in the case of the Caribbean region, probability sampling methods are quite often impractical because of the absence of databases or registries of live music stakeholders. Consequentially, there might be no sampling frames from which one can draw a random sample. Therefore, in the case of research on live music trade in the Caribbean, non-probability sampling methods might be more practical. Some of the non-probability methods of sampling could include the snowball or referral technique as well as the convenience sampling technique.

Snowball sampling refers to when each participant who is surveyed gives referrals of their peers to a researcher. The sequence of referrals results in an increased sample size, pretty much, like a snowball which grows larger as it collects snow while rolling down a slope. Convenience sampling, however, requires a researcher to frequent the venues or areas where their target respondents are normally present. Therefore, for studies on live music trade, recruiting survey participants at festivals, nightclubs, and concerts, for example, is a form of convenience sampling. The drawback of non-probability techniques, such as snowball and convenience sampling, are the increased risks of biases in the results which emerge from the survey. To avoid these biases, it is being recommended that an interval snowball sampling technique be used. This would require that several streams of contacts be surveyed to reduce the risk of sameness in responses because of familial or friendly connections among participants. The risk of biases can also be lessened when participants are screened for ensuring variations in age, gender, and levels of professional experience to reflect ample representativeness in the participants' responses.

Given the developments in information technology, researchers might wish to send out electronic surveys to respondents. However, this technique often yields poor response rates. It is therefore being advised that researchers either go out personally to survey participants or do so via videoconferencing platforms. While conducting face to face surveys on the ground or online, it is strongly recommended that electronic surveying platforms are used. These could ensure that at the stage of data transformation, the information collected could be easily exported to spreadsheets required for statistical analysis purposes rather than having to manually enter the data unto these spreadsheets.

Conclusion

For some in the Caribbean, and perhaps elsewhere in the world, the prospect of experimental research on cultural industries like live music might be daunting, especially within a context where the data is either lacking or non-existent. However, responding to a need for empirical data on a specific industry where that data is lacking can be a fulfilling venture. The process of sourcing primary data from live music stakeholders offers an excellent opportunity for researchers to build relationships with populations which are often hard-to-reach due to their touring and studio recording commitments. Furthermore, pursuing experimental studies of this nature can be a rewarding experience for researchers and the people for which their research is pertinent. In the Caribbean, for example, the region's urban and rural populations are heavily involved in the music industry. Therefore, as a researcher, doing your part to see how you can help these populations earn a lucrative living from their talent is a rewarding feeling like no other. And, from a scientific perspective, it is absolutely satisfying to see data which were collected from respondents, being transformed into quantifiable figures which are then statistically analysed. The suspense of not knowing what statistical outcomes may yield in terms of trends, correlations between variables and numbers, makes experimental studies on trade in cultural services like live music exciting.

Given the data driven world that we live in today, researchers from the Caribbean should be inspired to adopt more empirical approaches to studies on their region's entertainment services, especially in relation to international trade in live music. Currently, there is a preponderance of qualitative research on Caribbean creative and cultural industries. They have been highly beneficial to giving some insight into the challenges experienced by the Caribbean in the development of these industries, especially in relation to making Caribbean cultural/entertainment industries more globally competitive. However, arguably, empirical studies on Caribbean entertainment services trade will further enrich the body of knowledge within the field of Caribbean creative and cultural industries. Arguments over the pertinence of experimental approaches to studies on creative and cultural industries by some Caribbean researchers, who are advocates for qualitative approaches are counterproductive. After all, empirical approaches on studies on creative and cultural industries have already been used to good effect, by European researchers such as Rouet (2007/2015) and Hellmanzick and Schmitz (2016). Therefore, such disputes by Caribbean researchers on the suitability of empirical methodologies in the study of creative and cultural industries might retard the development of entertainment services in the region. It is essential to accept the importance of both research orientations and the fact that they complement each other. Acceptance that both qualitative and empirical research have their place in the study of creative and cultural industries, will ensure that one will have a more complete picture on international trade in Caribbean live music services.

The next chapters will present some of the findings from the Gordon (2021) study which used the proposed approach for an examination on interregional trade in live music between sovereign and non-sovereign states in the Caribbean. The findings from the Gordon (2021) study will be critically analysed to explore how they might relate to future studies on South-South and North-South interregional trade in Caribbean live music services. Therefore, the information contained in the next chapters could serve as inspiration to researchers looking for ideas on the kinds of variables they can explore when pursuing future experimental research on interregional trade in cultural services. The following chapters also include a policy dimension relating to the variables discussed in the following chapters. These discussions on public policy within these chapters include where necessary a comparative examination of other regional contexts where international trade in live music services has been lucrative. Through these policy discussions within the next chapters, it is hoped that it would stimulate constructive debate on how interested parties of the North and the South could improve the prospects for international trade in Caribbean live music services.

Notes

1 While pursuing research on live music trade between French Caribbean overseas departments and Independent Anglophone CARIFORUM countries, this author discovered that live music stakeholders from the French Caribbean overseas territories, had experiences of being overlooked by venues in mainland France or of not being adequately covered by French media when they held successful live performances on the mainland.
2 See "Factor Analysis" by Gorsuch (2015), "A Step-By-Step Guide to Exploratory Factor Analysis with SPSS" by Watkins (2021) and "Statistics in Plain English" by Urdan (2017).

References

Gordon, Lisa. 2021 (Submitted). *Doctoral Thesis: The Trade in Live Music Services between European Union French Caribbean Territories and Anglophone CARIFORUM Countries: The Case Study of Guadeloupe and Trinidad & Tobago.* St Augustine: The University of The West Indies, St Augustine Campus.

Gorsuch, Richard L. 2015. *Factor Analysis.* New York: Routledge.

Hellmanzick, Christiane, and Martin Schmitz. 2016. "The impact of cultural exceptions: audiovisual services trade and trade policy." *Applied Economics Letters* (Routledge) 23 (10): 695–700. doi:https://www.tandfonline.com/doi/full/10.1080/13504851.2015.1100244.

Linder, Staffan B. 1961. *An Essay on Trade and Transformation.* New York; Uppsala: John Wiley and Sons; Almqvist and Wiksell.

Maurin, Alain, and Patrick Watson. 2002. "Quantitative Modelling of the Caribbean Macroeconomy for Forecasting and Policy Analysis: Problems and Solutions." *Social and Economic Studies* (The University of the West Indies, Mona, Jamaica) 51: 1–47.

Rouet, Francois. 2007/2015. "Le flux d'echanges internationaux de biens et services culturels: determinants et enjeux." Edited by DEPS: (Departement des etudes de la prospective et des statistiques. *Culture Etudes CE-2007-1 et des Statistiques* (OpenEdition Books) CE-2007-1. doi:9782111398719.

Urdan, Timothy C. 2017. *Statisitcs in Plain English.* New York: Routledge.

Watkins, Marley W. 2021. *A step-by-step guide to exploratory factor analysis with SPSS.* New York: Routledge.

5 When Trade Facilitation Fails

Adopting the K-pop Export Approach to Caribbean Live Music

Trade Facilitation Is Not Working for International Trade in Caribbean Live Music

Trade facilitation measures are policies and programmes designed to overcome barriers to trade or stimulate trade growth. In the case of the Caribbean, the Economic Partnership Agreement (EPA) is a trade facilitation mechanism, since in theory, it is a bilateral agreement signed in 2008 to liberalise the flow of goods and services between territories of the EU and the CARIFORUM. Within this agreement, there is a protocol specifically focused on cultural services known as the Protocol of Cultural Cooperation. This protocol regulates non-monetary trade facilitation initiatives for entertainment services like live music. Therefore, cultural exchange programmes offered by tertiary education institutions, not-for-profit music festivals to expose foreign audiences to one's culture, and creative networking hubs for live music stakeholders from the respective regions to connect, are among some of the activities that would be permitted within this protocol. The objective of the Protocol of Cultural Cooperation is to use non-monetary means for creating an environment that would eventually lead to the development of monetary exchanges in cultural services between the EU and the CARIFORUM.

However, findings from a previous study on live music trade between the EU French Caribbean and Anglophone CARIFORUM countries revealed that the Economic Partnership Agreement and its protocol of cultural cooperation are trade facilitation measures which are having no significance on this trade Gordon (2021).[1] This is no surprise because the live music stakeholders who were surveyed gave an overall negative score for the impact that trade facilitation measures were having on this trade. They believed that Caribbean leadership was not doing enough to facilitate interregional live music trade between

DOI: 10.4324/9781003343325-5

the EU non-sovereign and CARIFORUM sovereign territories of the region Gordon (2021). These findings indicate that there is need to revolutionise the current measures to support the development of inter-regional trade in Caribbean live music. How can this be done? The answer may lie in the South Korean strategy for the export of their cultural services within the Asian-Pacific Region, Europe, and North America. Some may ask, why the South Korean model of live music trade is being used as a reference for the Caribbean in this book. South Korea has been chosen because it is perhaps one of the world's greatest success stories when it comes to the globalisation of its entertainment services. Despite non-tariff barriers like language differences, this country is arguably a heavy weight in international trade in entertainment services. This is quite an achievement when one considers that up to 2011, Korean live music possibly remained in obscurity, at least for extra-regional markets of the North. It is remarkable that within the period of some 11 years there has been both a high intraregional and extra-regional demand for this country's live music performances. Indeed, the South Korean success story suggests that its strategies for the development of trade in its live music are to be followed by regions such as the Caribbean, where the music (with the probable exclusion of reggae), is not consumed as much as the highly demanded live music from the North.

Adopting the South Korean Export Strategy for International Trade in Caribbean Live Music

The South Korean government invests heavily in strategies and programmes to facilitate the export of their cultural services like live K-pop music. Since the mid 1990's the Korean government began a systematic project of injecting capital into the development and export of their entertainment sector Kim (2018). It supports, for example, its Ministry of Culture in assisting the private sector in the development of cultural exports such as K-pop Kim (2018). It is estimated that the Korean government would have already made investments to the tune of over 900 million USD towards the international trade of K-pop (Na 2013 as cited in Kim 2018). These investments can sometimes take the form of subsidies, stimulus funds, low interest loans, and credit schemes. It also sponsors K-pop festivals held overseas via Korean embassies and cultural centres (Kim 2018). Among the festivals sponsored by the government include K-pop live music events held in Mexico, Paris, and Iran (Kim 2018).

The government's handsome investment in the development of its cultural exports is a purposeful strategy for the advancement of their foreign policy agenda. An agenda which Kim (2018) describes as being framed within the theory of "soft power".[2] "Soft power" is defined as the ability for a country to realise its policy agenda through persuasion rather than "coercion" (Nye 2004 and Snow 2014 as cited in Kim 2018). Simply put, rather than the use of military force and other hard-line foreign policy strategies such as economic sanctions, soft power requires a "kill 'em with kindness" approach to foreign policy. Therefore, cultural exports like live music constitute an important kind of soft power arsenal. Overtime, the expected outcome following the use of live music as a diplomatic tool is to inspire the citizenry of foreign nations to have a positive impression of the country which uses strategies of soft power.

The highly popular boy band BTS embodies South Korea's use of soft power. On June 1, 2022, the Korean group visited the White House to build awareness of anti-Asian racism in the United States (Cruz 2022). By the issue that they raised, on can glean that this is a priority problem which South Korea wishes to address on behalf of the East Asian diaspora in North America. It is said that the benefits of the soft power strategy are that it makes it easier for a county which uses it, to influence international action on its priority areas which could include strengthening international trade, sustainable development, and calling attention to racial marginalisation of diaspora populations as seen in the example of BTS' white house visit.

Would export measures premised on the soft power approach work for developing international trade in Caribbean live music services? The next section explores this.

Export of Caribbean live music using the Seoul Approach of "Soft Power"

Would the South Korean approach of merging export of live music with diplomacy work for the development of trade in Caribbean live music services? It just might.

By adopting this approach, Caribbean leadership would be able to fill two needs with one deed:

- Bring global attention to the issues which are of regional concern. These include but are not limited to climate change, food security, slum clearance, and health.
- Differentiate its live music offering within a highly competitive live music market.

The question, one would be surely asking at this point is how the Caribbean leadership can go about proceeding with this suggested initiative. The leadership can, for example, begin programmes and projects to encourage live performers to include Caribbean priority issues in the lyrics of their songs performed. In this vein, the region might be able to meet the demand of a certain demographic of concertgoers from the North and South who crave music with lyrical depth. It might be argued, however, that for many live music stakeholders in the region it might be a hard sell to channel their energies into producing and commercialising live music content of this nature, within a context where there is arguably an overwhelming global demand for contemporary music with lyrics for partying, freedom of sexuality and the glorification of violence. Nonetheless, it is being proposed that Caribbean leadership consider conducting experimental research to test the viability of merging live music trade strategies with its international relations priorities.

Integrating diplomatic priorities on social issues with international trade in live music services should not seem as otherworldly for the Caribbean. This is because there have already been Caribbean live performers who have appealed to consumers the world over through their socially conscious songs on issues such as environmental conservation, war, and racism. Jamaica's Bob Marley toured both cities of the North and South with his single "War" which spoke to issues on how the perpetuation of an ideology of the superiority of one race over another can produce war. British group of Jamaican ancestry, Steel Pulse with their live performance of "Earth Crisis" kept concertgoers riveted as they sung on the ravages of war on the natural environment. This is why, given this region's illustrious history of producing live music with depth, it is being proposed that more experimental research be done to see if joining diplomatic priorities on social issues with live music production, could facilitate the development of South-South and North-South trade in Caribbean live music services.

How the Caribbean Can Source Funding to Implement the South Korea Export Strategy

Measures of the kind used by South Korea for the export of entertainment services such as live music, require large sums of money. South Korea is reported to have spent over 900 million USD on K-pop export projects which include sponsoring overseas live music events, supporting the Korean entertainment private sector that contracts the services of foreign language songwriters, producers, and performers to develop a global demand for K-pop live music tours. However, in the Caribbean access to this amount of money for the development of creative industries like live music is not readily available. Even though, it was envisaged that the EU-CARIFORUM Economic Partnership Agreement would have reaped profitable dividends for both South-South and North-South interregional trade in entertainment services, this is not the reality. Therefore, Caribbean leaders might want to take more creative steps to encourage more international funding for projects aimed at developing trade in live music from the region. One step could be appealing to the region's live music stakeholders to create lyrical content that marries the developmental concerns of the EU with the diplomatic priorities of the Caribbean. In so doing, Caribbean leadership might offer a more convincing argument on why they should secure substantial EU funding for the development of interregional trade in live music. Indeed in these recent times where global financial resources are particularly scarce because of soaring energy prices, the COVID-19 pandemic aftershocks and Ukrainian-Russian war, international donors are likely more circumspect with their donations. Therefore, a proposed creative project which involves Caribbean live music stakeholders combining the region's pressing social-justice issues with that of the EU or other Northern nations, might persuade international donors to inject more funding towards the development of international trade in Caribbean live music services. Bilateral North-South negotiations on this matter ought to consider the cultural sensibilities of each region.

Zeroing in on the priority issues of the North would require in depth scholarly research and engagement. In the context of identifying the priority issues of Europe, for example, which is a continent that is richly heterogenous in languages and customs, academic engagement by Caribbean scholars who are proficiently multilingual with an interdisciplinary background would be required. Scholars of this kind would have the wherewithal to investigate priority issues of EU nations outlined in legislative documents, texts, documentaries, and televised panel discussions among experts. Such scholars would be equally equipped to engage with the EU society through delivery of lectures in the native language of an EU territory and through academic publications written in the country's native language. This kind of engagement would certainly help the Caribbean and specifically the independent Anglophone CARIFORUM countries, have a good grasp of the priorities of European nations. Thus, it would permit Caribbean researchers to advise as to how live music stakeholders should tailor their music to meet the pressing needs of EU metropoles, and as to how negotiations can be framed for more funding to support trade facilitation measures for the development of the Caribbean music industry.

Earlier in this book, for example, a parliamentary report published in French, referenced the French government's agenda for its overseas territories of the Americas. The first objective within this report was to use the overseas territories as a means of increasing the EU's global influence in the world. Therefore, Caribbean leadership of both independent and non-independent territories should consider researching how interregional live music trade can help the EU advance its foreign policy agenda or investigate what the priority issues of the EU's populace are. This suggestion relative to the populace is important because the populace can yield power to influence its leaders in framing both national and foreign policy initiatives. South Korea, it would seem, understands this. It is likely not a coincidence that Korean band BTS donated 1 million USD to Black Lives Matter (BLM). It is highly likely, South Korean leadership would have been the engine room behind this donation. The leadership of this East Asian country appears to have paid attention to the matters which were of import to the American populace, and would have been cognizant of the power which the populace yields in shaping the national and foreign policy agenda in the United States.

One observes, for example, that two years after the worldwide BLM protests against the heartless murder of Black American George Floyd by a White Police officer, there is arguably a more robust US policy for diversity. More universities, it would seem, are increasing access to scholarships and fellowships for candidates of either Asian or Black ancestry. There have been equally more national discussions on developing national policies to correct systemic economic disparities between Black and White Americans as it relates to access to housing, employment, business loans, and health. The US populace has seemingly influenced North-South international relations. Britain's Prince William on June 22, 2022 unveiled a statue erected in honour of the "Windrush" generation of Caribbean migrants who though having contributed enormously to the development of the United Kingdom were marginalised in British society. His father, Prince Charles during a Commonwealth meeting held in Rwanda on June 24th, 2022, indicated his readiness to discuss the enduring impact of the legacy of slavery. Similarly, the Royal family of Belgium returned some of the artifacts which their family pillaged from the Democratic Republic of Congo during their conquest of this central African state. Additionally, the European commission in the midst of anti-racism international protests following the murder of George Floyd, soon after, voted to formally recognise that the transatlantic slave trade and slavery constituted grave crimes against humanity. The above examples show that the national issues of one country have a domino effect on setting the foreign policy agenda of other countries.

And so, the takeaways from this discussion are as follows:

- Encourage Caribbean live performers to include in their lyrics, content which is pertinent to social issues of the North as well as the South.
- Investigate what the pressing issues of the North are through academic research and engagement.
- Deploy Caribbean researchers who are multilingual with an interdisciplinary background to conduct this research and academic engagement in the North.
- Conduct negotiations for implementing a "soft power" like strategy for the development of trade in Caribbean live music within a context where the cultural sensibilities of both the North and the South are respected.

How the WTO Can Support Trade Facilitation Measures for Interregional Trade in Caribbean Live Music

The above sections discussed how Caribbean leadership, through drawing inspiration from the South Korean approach can support the development of international trade in its live music services. This section suggests how the WTO (World Trade Organisation) can assist in the successful implementation of trade facilitation measures for interregional trade in Caribbean live music services.

Access to data on services like live music is an issue in the Caribbean region. It appears that the asynchronous approach of CARICOM member states regarding the implementation of the legal framework of the Caribbean Single Market and Economy (CSME), stipulated within the Revised Treaty of Chaguaramas (1989), which might have contributed to the incomplete status of the CSME project, could be the root cause of this data issue. Indeed, had the CSME project been fully completed, the outcome might have been the creation of a centralised database where regional information on cultural services trade could be stored and exchanged. Current data on Caribbean cultural industries and even other sectors, have been described by some previous scholars as being sporadic or anecdotal in nature. Many of these scholars are on the same page that the scarce data on cultural industries and particularly cultural services have arisen because of the following:

- **The invisibility of services trade** – Services are notoriously difficult to capture given its intangible nature as opposed to goods.
- **Low investment on data collection on cultural services** – cultural services like those of live music are increasingly difficult to capture given that many Caribbean islands give low priority towards investing in data collection on cultural services when compared to non-cultural services industries.
- **Deficiencies in existing data** – Maurin and Watson (2002) allude to economic data deficiency in the Caribbean stemming from the fact that the "data series required for a macroeconometric model of even the most modest size might be either non-existent or plagued by missing values, or too short or finally of inappropriate frequency." Maurin and Watson (2002) also note that the questionable quality of economic data in the Caribbean is a result of the time lag associated with the data collection processes.
- **Metropoles not disaggregating data** – Deficiencies in existing data within the Caribbean basin are further compounded by the fact that data in EU French Caribbean territories are not separated from that of mainland France. Former director of the Guadeloupean branch of SACEM, the foremost collection management organisation (CMO) of France, for example, informed that relative to their internal data on royalty inflows and outflows between their organisation and the CMOs of other countries, SACEM's data are supplied in aggregates, and they are not broken down into regions that reflect shares of royalties generated from the French Caribbean overseas territories.
- **No uniformity in data infrastructure** – Data collection is not uniform across the Caribbean region, thus making it difficult to interpret and analyse. The UNESCO Institute for Statistics (UIS), for example, states that because countries do not follow a uniformed approach to categorising a given cultural activity, this contributes to the WTO's "limited data at a detailed level Deloumeaux (2020)." This lack of uniformity in data capture practices makes it difficult to "assess the magnitude of international trade of cultural services Deloumeaux (2020)."

Without the required data for analysis on the volume of interregional trade in Caribbean live music or the factors impacting on this trade, it then becomes an onerous task to engage in evidence-based policymaking for developing this trade. Therefore, in this respect the WTO, given its trade facilitation mandate, could play an active role in supporting live music trade data collection initiatives in the Caribbean, as shall be explored in the next section.

The Structure and Functions of the World Trade Organisation

Prior to discussing how the World Trade Organisation (WTO) can facilitate interregional trade in Caribbean live music services, it is first important to remind readers of the structure and functions of this organisation. The WTO is a regulatory body founded in 1995. Headquartered in Geneva, Switzerland, it falls under the umbrella of the United Nations and comprises of over 160 member states. Its members are the only ones responsible for formulating policy for international trade. Actions taken with respect to policy on trade related issues and disputes are usually the outcome of meetings held among ministers of member-states, every two years. This is known as the Ministerial Conference, and it is the highest body of the WTO. Meetings are also held among the representatives of the diplomatic missions of these member countries. This is known as the General Council and unlike the Ministerial Conference, the council meets regularly. The General Council is comprised of sub-councils, among which includes the Council for Trade in Services. This council is charged with "facilitating the operation of the General Agreement on Trade in Services (GATS) and for furthering its objectives WTO (2022)." In addition, the council is "open to all WTO members and can establish subsidiary bodies as appropriate WTO (2022)." Now having already outlined the functions of the WTO, the next section investigates the pervasive problem of the alarming lack of data on Caribbean live music. This next section is important because it is the foundation on which recommendations are made in this chapter on how the WTO can facilitate international trade in Caribbean live music services, particularly, South-South interregional trade in the Caribbean.

The Challenge of Data: The Impediment for South-South Interregional trade in Caribbean Live Music

It would appear that despite having a council responsible for overseeing all matters related to international trade in services, the WTO seemingly has a challenge in collating data on cultural services trade such as live music, especially in relation to the ACP group (of which CARIFORUM countries are a subset), and the overseas territories of the EU. This is to be expected when one considers (as previously discussed) the data collection challenges on cultural industries within the Caribbean. The gaps in the WTO data which are seemingly the outcome of poor data collection infrastructure in regions of the South such as the Caribbean, are as follows:

• The WTO bulk data on export and import of cultural services are not disaggregated so that one can ascertain how much of them relate to music and particularly live music.

• The WTO data for ACP countries are not disaggregated so that one can identify the value of export and import of live music services in ACP countries like those of the Anglophone CARIFORUM.

• The WTO data for metropolitan European countries such as France are not disaggregated to determine how much certain EU overseas Caribbean territories contribute to the value of export and import in cultural services.

• Existing figures supplied by the WTO, do not reveal the trading relationships in cultural services between overseas EU Caribbean territories and ACP countries of which CARIFORUM is a subset.

Despite these problems in compiling data records for Caribbean cultural services faced by the WTO, this does not mean that they cannot be solved. Finding solutions to these problems are certainly of specific importance for developing nations of the Caribbean where young at-risk urban and rural populations are actively involved in the live music industry. If the entrepreneurial benefits of international trade are to be enjoyed by the Caribbean's at-risk youth, then more needs to be done to ensure that there are proper empirical records which document whether the region's indigent urban and rural young populations are adequately profiting from international trade in services in a way that could positively transform their quality of life. The following section, therefore, presents some recommendations that the WTO could consider implementing to address the dilemma of not having adequate records on trade in Caribbean cultural services industries. It is envisaged that if implemented by the WTO, meaningful development of both South-South and North-South interregional trade in Caribbean live music could ensue.

How WTO can support Development of South-South Interregional Trade in Caribbean Live Music

To address the issue of data paucity on South-South interregional trade in Caribbean live music services, the WTO's Council for Trade in Services, can set up a "Committee on Trade in Cultural Services". The functions of this proposed committee should be as follows:

- Have discussions on cultural services trade-related matters. The committee should also offer proposals for the Council on Trade in Services to address the urgent matter of data collection on cultural services like live music. The recommended committee on trade in cultural services, for example, could facilitate discussions and negotiations on funding the project of a centralised data system within the Caribbean (and other ACP regions).
- Present proposals on the kind of technical support that the Caribbean would require for the completion of this centralised data system project. This technical support could include hiring multilingual research consultants with expertise in statistical modelling and international trade theory. This is because they would be able to design an empirical research approach that would be applicable to investigating the challenges faced by central statistical offices of the Caribbean in collecting and analysing data on cultural services trade like live music.

How the WTO Can Support the Development of North-South Interregional Trade

The above recommendations were made with specific reference to how the WTO could support the development of South-South interregional trade in Caribbean live music services. Suggestions on how this organisation can support North-South interregional trade are listed below:

- The proposed WTO "Committee for Trade in Cultural Services" could form an "EU-CARIFORUM bilateral oversight agency" comprising of multilingual international trade representatives of these regional trading blocs. This suggested bilateral oversight agency should be managed by the WTO. The proposed primary function of this oversight agency should be to annually monitor how CARIFORUM countries and EU countries are implementing their laws and policies for the trade in cultural services such as live music via the GATS 4 modes of trade.
- The proposed "EU-CARIFORUM cultural services oversight agency" could regularly evaluate the efficiency of the local laws on the GATS modes of trade in both EU and CARIFORUM countries, especially in relation to mode 4 (movement of natural

persons) and mode 2 (consumption abroad) – the traditional modes which support the sustainable exchange in live music services.

- The oversight agency should also look into strengthening possibilities of mode 1 (cross-border trade). Strengthening cross-border trade is particularly important currently when one considers how advancements in ICT continue to transform creative industries. The many livestreamed pay-per-view music performances during the pandemic have shown how live music services trade has leapfrogged into the virtual space.
- The oversight agency should conduct empirical studies using primary data sourced directly from the region's live music stakeholders to find out the degree to which they have been benefitting from live music trade via the GATS 4 modes of trade. The WTO can provide the oversight agency with the requisite human resources of multilingual international trade specialists to support these empirical activities.

Conclusion

It is important to understand that results from export strategies and trade facilitation measures for the development of trade in Caribbean live music services might not happen as quickly as one would hope. South Korea, for example, despite having injected a handsome amount of capital for development and export initiatives of its entertainment services since the 1990's, had only begun reaping the fruits of its labour and investment, approximately 20 years later. Therefore, export and trade facilitation measures for the development of international trade in Caribbean live music would require sustained funding and commitment before bearing abundant fruit for the region.

Notes

1 Key findings from the Gordon (2021) study on the impact of the Economic Partnership Agreement (EPA) on live music trade between the EU French Caribbean and Anglophone CARIFORUM revealed that the volume of trade in live music services between the EU French Caribbean and Anglophone CARIFORUM is low. The mean value for the volume of trade in live music services between the two territories following regression analysis was 1.86. This mean value was based on the EFA subset of 5 questions used in regression to measure this variable. This result suggests that the Economic Partnership Agreement (EPA) has not significantly increased the volume of trade in live music services between these territories. Among the factors contributing to this is the fact that the non-commercial

programmes and projects encouraged through the EPA's Protocol on Cultural Cooperation, aimed at facilitating reciprocal market access for cultural service providers from both EU and CARIFORUM regions, are not having a positive impact on live music trade between Guadeloupe and Trinidad & Tobago. Findings from the descriptive statistics revealed that both Guadeloupean and Trinidadian live music stakeholders believe that training and other non-commercial programmes such as publicly funded workshops and business to business networking events are not adequately helping them gain access to each other's markets. When asked to give a score on how they believed non-commercial programmes such as those listed above, were facilitating live music trade, Guadeloupeans and Trinidadians rated these negatively by attributing scores of 2.32 and 2.74.

Another reason why trade facilitation measures as those prescribed under the EPA are not having a significant impact on increasing the volume of live music trade between the two territories is that commitments relative to Mode 4 (touring) are not being adequately applied. Music stakeholders from both territories, for example, did not believe that their countries' immigration laws sufficiently facilitated the temporary stay of artistes from their respective regions, with those from Guadeloupe attributing a negative score of 2.73 and those from Trinidad & Tobago 2.95.

The Economic Partnership Agreement stipulates that cultural service providers of both EU and CARIFORUM regions would only be permitted to contractually work in the other's territory provided that they are formally registered in their countries of origin. Yet the findings showed that formally registered music stakeholders from Guadeloupe and Trinidad & Tobago were not gaining access to each other's markets. It appears that this is the case because more needs to be done to make the artist registries of live music stakeholders accessible in the other's territory. When asked to rate whether a registry which lists artistes from the other's territory is easily accessed, both Guadeloupean and Trinidadian music stakeholders attributed negative scores of 2.27 and 2.03. Similarly, relative to the statement inquiring whether registries listing promoters from the other territory is accessible, music stakeholders from Guadeloupe and Trinidad and Tobago also gave this statement negative ratings of 2.23 and 2.18.

The findings also revealed that the EPA has not permitted music stakeholders to adequately maximise the geographic closeness between the two territories, thus accounting for why this agreement has not had a significant impact on increasing the volume of live music trade. Live music stakeholders when asked to rate whether they believed the EPA worked in terms of freeing trade to bridge the distance between Guadeloupe and Trinidad & Tobago caused by Guadeloupe's status as an EU territory, both Guadeloupeans and Trinidadians attributed negative scores of 2.73 and 2.26. These findings concerning the EPA are unfortunate given that the regression results showed that the geographic proximity between the countries is the most significant of all the variables in relation to live music trade.

2 Kim (2018) credits Nye (2009) for having invented this term.

References

Chapelier, Annie, and Berangere Peletti. 2020. *Rapport d'information sur l'environnement international des departements et collectivites d'outre-mer.* Parliamentary Report, Paris: Assemblee Nationale.

Cruz, Lenika. 2022. "BTS Gets It." *The Atlantic*, 7 June. https://www.theatlantic.com/culture/archive/2022/06/bts-white-house-visit-aapi-inclusion/661206/.

Deloumeaux, Lydia. 2020. "Trade in Cultural Services Statistics." *Joint ECLAC and UNSD Workshop in cooperation with WTO on Trade in Services.* Accessed December 2021.

Gordon, Lisa. 2021 (Submitted). *Doctoral Thesis: The Trade in Live Music Services between European Union French Caribbean Territories and Anglophone CARIFORUM Countries: The Case Study of Guadeloupe and Trinidad & Tobago.* St Augustine: The University of The West Indies, St Augustine Campus.

Kim, Hun-Shik. 2018. *When Diplomacy Faces Trade Barriers and Diplomatic Frictions: The Case of the Korean Wave.* Vol. 14, in *Place Branding and Public Diplomacy.* Macmillan Publishers Ltd.

Maurin, Alain, and Patrick Kent Watson. 2002. "Quantitative Modelling of the Caribbean Macroeconomy for Forecasting and Policy Analysis: Problems and Solutions." *Social and Economic Studies* (The University of the West Indies, Mona) 51: 5–6.

Nurse, Keith, and Alicia Nicholls. 2011. *Enhancing Data Collection in the Creative Industries Sector in CARIFORUM.* Inter-Agency Presentation: ITC, UNCTAD, WTO and WIPO, Georgetown: Shridath Ramphal Centre for International Trade Law, Policy and Services.

The World Trade Organization. n.d. *The World Trade Organization.* Accessed August 2022. https://www.wto.org/english/thewto_e/gcounc_e/gcounc_e.htm.

6 Overcoming Cultural Issues in International Trade in Caribbean Live Music

The K-pop Strategy

Interregional live music trade in the Caribbean is quite often looked at through the lens of cultural proximity. Simply put, cultural proximity refers to the similarities in culture that one country has with another. This cultural proximity can be manifested in shared history, demographics, cuisine, dance, music, and, of course, language. The Caribbean region because of the historical leitmotif of European conquest and colonialism is a region often thought of as being comprised of territories with strong cultural commonalities. However, sometimes, it would appear, that despite these commonalities, this does not always translate into positive outcomes for live music trade. Take, for example, the EU French Caribbean overseas territory of Guadeloupe and the Anglophone CARIFORUM country of Trinidad & Tobago. These are two territories which share commonalities in French colonialism, the enslavement of Africans and East Indian indentureship. These similarities are borne out in food, religion, surnames, folkloric tales, the everyday vernacular of French creole, and even the similar phenotypical appearance of inhabitants which are reflective of the historical migratory patterns of these regions. Yet, for all these apparent cultural similarities, statistical modelling showed that culture has not impacted positively on this trade (Gordon 2021).[1] Why was this the case? The descriptive data from the Gordon (2021) study showed that the difference in the official languages between Guadeloupe and Trinidad and Tobago had a far too negative impact on live music trade between the two territories to the extent of undermining all the other cultural similarities shared by them.

The case of Guadeloupe and Trinidad & Tobago, therefore, shows that similarities in culture do not always equal positive outcomes for interregional trade. Therefore, when it comes to harnessing culture for the development of live music trade, a well-thought-out strategy is required. South Korea can serve as a reference for how this can

DOI: 10.4324/9781003343325-6

be done. It is a country that has had experience with cultural similarities not boding well for intraregional trade in live music services with countries like Japan. This South Korean strategy as well as other issues will be addressed in the next section.

When Similarities in Culture Breed Animosities in Trade: South Korean Live Music in Japan

Those who are unfamiliar with East Asian history often make the flawed assumption that the high demand for South Korean K-pop in neighbouring markets like Japan is largely because East Asian countries share cultural commonalities. Nothing could be further from the truth. In the case of South Korea and Japan, cultural similarities have reduced Japanese demand for South Korean entertainment services like live K-pop music. This is because South Korea and Japan share a turbulent past that has been the source of great bilateral antagonism that persists even today. The animosity between the two countries is largely due to the Japanese occupation of Korea. The cultural friction between the two countries, resulting from historical tensions, is the very reason why South Korea has had to devise effective strategies to overcome them when trading their entertainment services in Japan. The source of these bilateral tensions will be elaborated upon, below.

Shared History: The Source of the South Korean-Japanese Impasse

Japan's imperial rule of South Korea from 1910 to 1945 has caused a great deal of angst among the South Korean population. South Koreans, it is said, feel tremendous resentment towards the Japanese. They believe that Japan remains unrepentant for the crimes against South Koreans during its occupation of the Korean Peninsula. During the early 20th century, the Japanese conquered and colonised the Korean people by forcibly enlisting Korean men to serve in the army during the Second World War and enslaving approximately 200,000 Korean women and girls into prostitution for the benefit of Japanese soldiers. These victims were termed as "comfort women". It is said that it is precisely this historical aspect of forced prostitution of Korean women which has influenced the contemporary strained relations between South Korea and Japan. South Koreans dissatisfied with the level of Japan's atonement for the sin of the sexual exploitation of Korean women, today, continue to advocate for reparative justice. However,

Japanese leadership has concluded that it has sufficiently made mone-tary amends for its colonial crimes since the signing of the 1965 Treaty on Basic Relations. Following this agreement Japan has supplied to South Korea grants valued today at 2.4 billion USD (Phillips, Lee and Yi 2020).

The shared bitter colonial history of South Korea and Japan has undoubtedly influenced how the respective populations perceive each other. South Koreans and their diaspora when polled on the trustwor-thiness of the Japanese gave their neighbours a low score of 4.3 on a scale from 0 to 10 (Phillips, Lee and Yi 2020). Similarly, the Japanese do not regard the South Koreans favourably. A public opinion poll conducted in 2014 revealed that over 66 percent of Japanese citizens over the age of 20 years feel they share no affinity with South Korea (Kim 2018). The findings from this poll might have arisen because the two populations' perceptions of the history these two countries share, are at variance. Generally, South Koreans are dissatisfied with the level of reparative justice they have received from the Japanese, whereas many of the Japanese populace believe that their country has done more than enough to compensate South Korea. It has even been reported that some Japanese deny that atrocities were ever meted out by Japan against South Koreans during Japanese imperialism (Phillips, Lee and Yi 2020). Consequentially, the difference in per-ceptions of the common history between the two nations would have arguably threatened the development of intraregional live music trade, had it not been for the proactive measures taken by South Korea's entertainment think tank. These proactive measures will be discussed in the next section.

The South Korean Culture Offensive to Win Japanese Favour for Live K-pop

It was previously discussed that cultural similarities between South Korea and Japan have had a negative impact on intraregional trade in Korean live music services to Japan. The shared violent past between the two countries, no doubt, has accounted for why, for a long time, the Japanese considered the consumption of South Korean entertain-ment as unpatriotic (Kim 2018). Seemingly, with the intent of over-coming this hurdle of contentious feelings because of the bitter history between the two countries, the South Korean entertainment conglom-erates with the assistance of the government have taken proactive measures to develop intraregional trade with Japan in entertainment services like live K-pop music. These measures are as follows:

- Ensuring that K-pop band members become proficient in Japanese (St. Michel 2011). A useful skill for talk show television appearances in Japan.
- Incorporating Japanese lyrics in K-pop songs (St. Michel 2011).
- Westernising the music performed by using the services of American producers (St. Michel 2011). This might have been a strategy used, given the universal appreciation of Western sounds, but it might have also been used as a way to "de-Koreanize" music, so that it became more pleasing to Japanese audiences.
- Recruiting foreigners of different East Asian heritage. This strategy might serve to elicit from the Japanese audience more positive feelings towards K-pop music given that some of the live performers are non-Korean.
- Sexualisation of K-pop female live performers in keeping with the universal belief that sex sells (St. Michel 2011).

These strategies seemingly have worked in mitigating the negative impact that the bitter history between these two neighbouring countries might have had on the profitable outcome of K-pop live music exports into Japan. The above strategies, it would appear, have even helped South Korea stave off the potential for a waning Japanese demand for K-pop live music because of an increased anti-Korean sentiment stemming from contemporary land disputes between the two nations, as well as Japan's fears about South Korea's diplomatic rapprochement with dictatorship led North Korea. Kim (2018), for example, reports that despite a growing anti-Korean sentiment in Japan since 2012, stemming from strengthened South and North Korean diplomacy, Japanese fans, particularly those of the younger generation, continued to attend live K-pop events (Kim 2018).

The South Korean context of exporting live K-pop to Japan has shown that even when cultural proximity between neighbouring nations is not always advantageous to trade, the issue can be overcome provided that proactive measures are implemented. Does this mean, therefore, that in the Caribbean where there are instances of cultural similarities not translating into increased interregional trade between neighbours that the above South Korean strategy would be applicable? This question will be explored in the next section.

The K-pop Culture Template for Interregional Trade in Caribbean Live Music

It was illustrated that the commonalities in culture between South Korea and Japan are not beneficial for interregional live music trade between the two countries. The case is similar between Caribbean sub-regions which adhere to different geopolitical frameworks. Although the sovereign and non-sovereign Caribbean territories share the common thread of European conquest and colonialism that have shaped a common Caribbean culture that in theory should translate into increased South-South interregional trade in Caribbean live music services, the reality is not the case. Trade volumes in entertainment services, particularly between the overseas French Caribbean territories and Anglophone CARIFORUM remain low. Findings from the Gordon (2021) study following statistical regression showed that the common culture between the EU French Caribbean territories and the Anglophone CARIFORUM states are not having a positive impact on trade in live music services. Therefore, would the South Korean model used to export its live music to Japan work in the Caribbean context? It might, and this shall now be discussed.

Despite the historical and socio-demographic similarities between the EU French Caribbean and Anglophone CARIFORUM, many consumers know very little about the other because they have not been sufficiently exposed to the culture of the other. In one of the earlier chapters, it was referenced how certain French academics like Taglioni (1997) believe that France has deliberately isolated its French Caribbean territories from forming meaningful diplomatic ties with their Anglophone sovereign neighbours. It was posited that this was done through fostering in their former Caribbean colonies, a dependency syndrome of turning to Mainland France to fulfil their socio-economic needs. As such, the impact of the dependency syndrome is that the EU French Caribbean territories do not see an urgent need to be proficient in English, the language of their sovereign neighbours who make up most of the region. If there is merit to this claim, it would then explain why despite other cultural commonalities between the two Caribbean sub-regions, the cultural hurdles generated by the reciprocal ignorance of their official languages, remain in place. So, what then, how can this language issue be addressed, using the South Korean paradigm? This will now be explored.

How Best to Apply the South Korean Template to Overcome the Language Issues for Trade in Caribbean Live Music

The importance of overcoming the language barriers between the sovereign and non-sovereign Caribbean states cannot be overstated. These barriers are not only a serious hindrance to the development of both South-South interregional trade but also North-South trade in Caribbean live music services. Language barriers might even be a serious obstacle in the development of trade in other kinds of non-cultural services from the Caribbean. Therefore, overcoming these language barriers are a must, and to do so would require sustained commitment, activism, and investment by Caribbean leaders. In an effort to overcome these barriers, it is being suggested that Caribbean leaders take inspiration from the approach used by the South Korean government, which, in calling for a rigorous campaign of foreign language immersion for its live performers, put its proverbial money where its mouth is by heavily funding language immersion programmes and other cultural rapprochement programmes. It is hence being recommended, that a fund be specifically allocated to addressing gaps related to language and other cultural issues which are thwarting the development of international trade in Caribbean live music. This fund should pay attention to financing the following proposed programmes.

Language Immersion Activities and Cross-Cultural Song Writing Camps

Language exchange programmes and cross-cultural language song-writing camps for Caribbean live music stake holders should be sponsored and organised. These programmes should be of a duration of no less than six months for each cohort of live music stakeholders. This is because language experts have observed that six months is a reasonable period for one who has no prior knowledge of a language, to become adequately proficient. These language immersion activities and cross-cultural song writing camps would function as creativity spaces for EU overseas territories and CARIFORUM countries of the Caribbean to network and listen to each other's music in order to increase bilateral music collaborations. A Trinidadian music manager posited that if emerging sovereign and non-sovereign Caribbean artistes, specialising in various genres of music were given a creativity space to listen to each other's works, they would be able to decide with whom they "vibe best" for a potential collaboration. Collaborations of this nature could mean that live music stakeholders from the EU overseas and independent countries of the Caribbean will expand consumer demand for their live music services by gaining reciprocal market access to the other's fanbase within the Caribbean and the diaspora communities across North America and Europe. The organisers of these language immersion and cross-cultural song-writing camps could be the collective management organisations (CMOs) which already have a vast membership of live music stakeholders.

Contracting Services of Caribbean Producers and Songwriters Who Are Native English, French and Dutch Speakers

The proposed language immersion fund should also be used to contract song-writing services of music stakeholders who are native speakers of either English, French or Dutch. Lyrics in the native Caribbean language of the other would ensure that Caribbean consumers who do not share the native language of a Caribbean artiste will understand what is being sung, thus contributing to the development of South-South interregional demand for Caribbean live music services. This strategy might also bode well in building an extra-regional demand for Caribbean live music services in North America and Europe where Caribbean diaspora populations reside. This strategy of recruiting foreign producers and songwriters is used by entertainment companies in South Korea. These South Korean entertainment companies are heavily subsidised by their government to recruit songwriters and producers from the United States (Lee 2020)."

Institutional Sponsorship for Staging of Live Music Events for Cross-Cultural Exposure Purposes

South Korea has employed the strategy of funding of live music events staged by its embassies and cultural centres in host nations located in the North and the South. The South Korean government, for instance, sponsored several K-pop festivals around the world which featured artists from South Korea and the host nation, through Korean embassies, media houses, and cultural centres (Kim 2018). This strategy was developed to commercialise K-pop to parts of the world where South Korea had low levels of cultural proximity (Kim 2018). Therefore, Caribbean leaders of sovereign and non-sovereign territories could fund their embassies and cultural centres representing their sub-regions, located in the Caribbean, as well as in North America and Europe to host live music events featuring artists from the host nation and their country. Funding these kinds of cultural exposure events is an investment that might produce dividends for the development of South-South and North-South interregional trade in Caribbean live music services.

Concentration on Diaspora Consumers

In an effort to overcome the language issue, South Korea has sought the assistance of East Asian populations in the North and in the South to promote trade in Korean live music. Presumably, the East Asian diaspora populations are used because of their assumed bilingual proficiency in Korean and the language of their host country. Therefore, it is expected that their language skills make them excellent informal ambassadors of Korean entertainment services who can influence their non-East Asian peers to appreciate live K-pop. This strategy has reaped dividends, as many marvel on the remarkable rise in the popularity of K-pop in North America and Europe without knowing that East Asian immigrant communities in these parts of the world were responsible for this (Kim 2018).[2]

This South Korean approach appears compatible within the Caribbean context of live music trade, to overcome language barriers through diaspora populations in South-South and North-South interregional markets. For example, in the case of North-South interregional markets, first-generation Caribbean migrant populations, educated in the language of the country of their birth, as well as the language of their immigrant parents, develop a proficiency in bilingual skills. Therefore, they can be excellent ambassadors for the marketing of Caribbean live music to their non-Caribbean peers of the North. For instance, to first-generation Guadeloupean-Americans attending colleges in the the United States could be recruited as influencers to promote live music services of the EU French Caribbean within this Anglophone North-American country via social media platforms such as Tik Tok, Instagram, and the like. Similarly, first generation St Lucians and Dominicans attending universities in Paris, Brussels, and Switzerland can be invited to serve as influencers of Caribbean live music services in these European cities.

Even European-based entertainment companies, it would seem, have been inspired by the South Korean approach of using diaspora markets to overcome language barriers and expand consumer demand for their live performers' music. The president of Warner music France, Thierry Chassagne states that the break-out success of Malian/French hip-hop artiste Aya Nakamura was partly due to the Caribbean and

African communities in Europe. Warner France, taking note of the enthusiasm of Caribbean and African diaspora populations in France to Nakamura's album, began searching for trade expansion prospects within diaspora populations outside of France. This was an effective strategy by the recording company because EU interregional demand for her music grew in non-Francophone countries such as Germany, Sweden, Portugal, Spain, Romania, Greece, Belgium, and Switzerland – proof of the power of the diaspora to create buzz despite language barriers.[3]

Caribbean Broadcast Media Support to Promote Caribbean Music

South Korean television station KBS has sponsored live music concerts featuring performers from South Korea and the host country. Therefore, one sees how the media has a primordial role in supporting live music trade by influencing consumer demand despite language barriers. Consequently, Caribbean media should be inspired by this South Korean approach. EU French Caribbean artistes such as Guadeloupean musicians Jacob Desvarieux (deceased) and Fred Deshayes have called for more support from the radio stations of CARIFORUM countries like Trinidad & Tobago to do their part in exposing EU French Caribbean music to listeners of the twin-island republic. Desvarieux (2019), for example, lamented about the Anglophone culture of having foreign artistes lobby and pay to have their music aired. This Anglophone media culture, he said, has turned off French musicians from exploring export possibilities for their live music services in CARIFORUM countries like Trinidad &Tobago. As such, it is essential that the media of sovereign and non-sovereign Caribbean territories realise their importance in fostering interregional and extra-regional consumer demand for Caribbean live music services. The Caribbean media of sovereign and non-sovereign territories must collectively brainstorm on innovative ways they can work together to develop this demand.

One-Stop Entertainment Management Companies

For some, the formation of one-stop entertainment management companies might be a controversial measure to address the barrier of language differences concerning trade in Caribbean live music. However, if Caribbean public institutions are looking for sure-fire means to guarantee the sustainable profitability of trade in the region's live music, even in the midst of language issues, measures must be implemented to ensure that the quality of Caribbean live music services remains consistently high for both South-South and North-South interregional consumption. A one-stop entertainment management company might be able to meet this need. These companies could be modelled to a limited degree after the highly controversial entertainment conglomerates in South Korea. However, if the Caribbean were to form companies of this nature, due caution must be exercised to safeguard against repressing the creativity and preserving the independence of live music stakeholders. If these proposed one-stop entertainment-management companies are not adequately policed, Caribbean live music stakeholders can run the risk of being victims of entrepreneurial exploitation by companies. It has been argued, for example, that these companies are predatory by having their artistes sign contracts which are detrimental to the rights of the artistes and their creativity (Howard 2014).[4]

Notwithstanding these flaws in the South Korean entertainment management system of creating international demand for K-pop live music despite language barriers, certain observers see positive qualities in the South Korean entertainment management style. These observers attribute the international success of K-pop to its business model of centralised entertainment production companies because it is a model which minimises the costs involved in commercialising live music internationally. These costs are minimised because South Korean entertainment management companies function as a one-stop enterprise. These companies are comprised of individual private firms which specialise in a given entertainment commercial service. Therefore, within these Korean entertainment companies there is a division responsible for talent scouting, another for human resource operations, and an additional entity for styling artistes. Furthermore, within these Korean entertainment companies there is a firm responsible for the management of artistes, another for song-writing and music production and an additional entity in charge of media promotion (Khieum 2013 as cited in Howard 2014). These entertainment companies where entertainment export preparation services are centralised have been credited for the success in the export of K-pop in regional Asian markets and external North American/European markets. They ensure that K-pop live performers maintain a consistent quality in their sound, appearance, and dance choreography.

Notwithstanding, the resounding success of the role these one-stop entertainment companies play in the internationalisation of K-pop live music, it is being recommended that the Caribbean adopt this model but be very cautious in doing so, fully cognizant of the negative aspects of this model. The positive result from adopting the South Korean model, despite its negative aspects, could be the reduction of the costs involved in the development of international demand for Caribbean live music. This could mean that the region's emerging artists (and other live music stakeholders) will have access to the same export preparation services as the region's established live music stakeholders who can independently afford them.

Conclusion

In this chapter one discovered that cultural commonalties do not always guarantee increased trade in services such as live music, for a variety of reasons. Among the reasons which diminish the positive impact of cultural similarities between nations are language differences. However, based on the tremendous strides made by South Korea to develop international trade in its live music services, despite issues like language barriers, the Caribbean region can see that this language bogeyman can be conquered. All it takes is a South Korean-like systematic and sustained approach to defeat this challenge. That said, before adopting the South Korean approach of overcoming cultural challenges like language barriers, it is being strongly suggested that researchers first conduct experimental studies on how best to implement this approach for the development of international trade in Caribbean live music services.

Notes

1 The author conducted an experimental study on South-South interregional trade in live music services between the EU French Caribbean territories and Anglophone CARIFORUM countries. The results emerging from that study on culture were quite unexpected. It turned out that the p-value of .468 suggested that similarities in culture between the two countries were not having a significant impact on the volume of trade in live music. This result reflects to a certain degree that of Roue (2007/2015)'s study, where it was shown that cultural considerations such as common language and common colonial histories could have no impact on international trade in cultural services between France and OECD countries. However, what was even more astonishing relative to the study on Guadeloupe and Trinidad &Tobago is that the Pearson Correlation value of −.013 associated with the variable of culture indicated that similarities in culture are having a negative impact on the volume of trade in live music services between the EU French Caribbean territories and Anglophone CARIFORUM countries.

2 See Kim (2018) for more information.
3 Alain Veille, Managing Director of Digital Warner Music France describes the strategy of targeting diaspora markets for Nakamura's international success. He states that his team's strategy in the surrounding territories was foremost to develop a fanbase among her community prior to building awareness of her music among the general population.
4 Howard (2014), in describing the conditions imposed by South Korean entertainment management companies, relates that there have been harsh contractual arrangements which have in some cases, bound K-pop artistes to these companies for a duration of 13 years, thus leaving these artistes vulnerable to exploitation.

References

Desvarieux, Jacob, interview by Lisa Gordon. 2019. *Personal Interview* (24 August).
Gordon, Lisa. 2021 (Submitted). *Doctoral Thesis: The Trade in Live Music Services between European Union French Caribbean Territories and Anglophone CARIFORUM Countries: The Case Study of Guadeloupe and Trinidad & Tobago.* St Augustine: The University of The West Indies, St Augustine Campus.
Howard, Keith. 2014. "Mapping K-Pop Past and Present: Shifting the Modes of Exchange." *Korea Observer* (ProQuest Central) 45 (3): 389–413.
Kim, Hun-Shik. 2018. *When Diplomacy Faces Trade Barriers and Diplomatic Frictions: The Case of the Korean Wave.* Vol. 14, in *Place Branding and Public Diplomacy.* Macmillan Publishers Ltd.
Lee, Alicia. 2020. "You know your K-pop stars. Now meet the American producers and songwriters behind them." *CNN Wire Service*, 29 March: 1–5.
Phillips, Joe, Wondong Lee, and Joseph Yi. 2020. "Future of South Korea–Japan Relations: Decoupling of Liberal Discourse." *The Political Quarterly* (Political Quarterly Publishing Company) 91 (2): 448–455. doi:10.1111/1467-923X.12786.
Rouet, Francois. 2007/2015. "Le flux d'echanges internationaux de biens et services culturels: determinants et enjeux." Edited by DEPS (Departerment des etudes de la prospective et des statistiques). *Culture Etudes CE-2007-1 et des Statistiques* (Open Edition Books) CE-2007-1 doi: 9782111398719.
St. Michel, Patrick. 2011. "How Korean Pop Conquered Japan." *The Atlantic*, 13 September. https://www.theatlantic.com/entertainment/archive/2011/09/how-korean-pop-conquered-japan/244712/.
Taglioni, Francois. 1997. "L'Association des Etats de la Caraibe dans les processus d'integration regionale." *Annales d'Amerique Latine et des Caraibes (HAL)* 14–15: 147–167.

7 Race & Ethnicity and International Trade in Caribbean Live Music

Why Exploring This Nexus Is Important

Introduction

An analysis of race and ethnicity within a paradigm of international trade might be an anomaly for some. However, such an approach to the analysis of economic related matters is nothing new or unusual. Research of this nature was first formalised by Jewish American economist, Gary Becker. In 1954, he conceptualised the theory: the Economics of Discrimination. His motivation for creating this theory was to investigate how racial discrimination would impact on the economic well-being of both its perpetrators and sufferers. Therefore, when applying his theory, he merged it with statistical modelling techniques so that he could have explored when the effects of racial discrimination perpetrated by some White-owned businesses tended to be most insidious for Black and Jewish Americans (Lazear 2015). In the case of international trade in Caribbean live music services, investigating the impact of racial discrimination is pertinent. Discovery of this was made during field research for the Gordon (2021) study, investigating interregional trade in Caribbean live music services.

Reasons for Studying Impact of Race and Ethnicity on International Trade in Caribbean Live Music

Many researchers might attest to instances of discovering new data, which require further investigation, while out on the field. However, immediate examination of these new findings while pursuing field studies are not always practical. This is especially true when the requisite financial resources and time for the prolongation of the research, are unavailable. This was alas, the case relative to the Gordon (2021) study on live music trade between EU French Caribbean territories

DOI: 10.4324/9781003343325-7

and Anglophone CARIFORUM countries. It turned out that race and ethnicity were new factors to be investigated for studies on international trade in Caribbean live music services. This is because anecdotal accounts by music stakeholders from the both the EU French Caribbean and the Independent English-speaking Caribbean states of the CARIFORUM suggest that their race and ethnicity have had a negative impact on their ability to export their live music services to the markets of the North, as shall now be described.

EU French Caribbean territories like Guadeloupe and Martinique are within a state of hybridity on the question of their trade with Europe. They are, by virtue of being overseas regions of the French Republic, intraregional trade partners within continental France and consequentially, the European Union, however, residents of these overseas territories, would often share, that in practice they are not treated as French but as "others" who do not truly belong to France. Martiniquan artiste E.SY Kennenga relates in song, his experience of this kind of discrimination. In one of his songs, for example, he describes feeling like an illegitimate child of a mother country which does not respect the creole language of his island of origin and expects him to assimilate into the majority culture at the expense of his French West Indian cultural identity (Gomez 2011). Others may rebut these assertions made by Kennenga by alluding to the tremendous success that Jamaican reggae/dancehall artistes enjoy in the North despite the use of their creole and references to their unique experiences and culture in their music.

Notwithstanding the success of some Jamaican live performers, many artistes from the Anglophone CARIFORUM and their diaspora also feel alienated within the live music industry of North America and Europe. British Jamaican comedian, Sir Lenny Henry, for example, in a rather tactful manner drew reference to the alienation of Black and Asian people (many of whom are of Caribbean origin) at the UK live music festival in Glastonbury. He bemoaned the absence of diversity at these festivals (Wright 2022). Lenny's observations on the seeming exclusion of people of colour at the Glastonbury festival are also supported by Indo-British musician Nitin Sawhney. Sawhney alleged in 2013, that Glastonbury organisers would customarily relegate him to "a minor stage" because of his race (ZEE News 2013). In the next section, one will learn more from the Caribbean musicians as they share their experiences of feeling marginalised in the markets of the North. Their accounts certainly underscore the importance of pursuing future experimental studies on the impact of race and ethnicity in the international trade of Caribbean live music.

The Commercial Impact of Race and Ethnicity on Caribbean Live Music Stakeholders in the North

Guadeloupean jazz musician Jacques Schwarz-Bart is a saxophonist with an impressive resume. He has worked with the likes of American jazz artiste Roy Hargrove. He has also worked with American Neo-Soul artiste D'Angelo (Delhaye 2018). Yet, despite his professional accomplishments, Schwarz-Bart, and others like him, are finding it difficult to trade their services in their European metropole. He perceives, for example, a sort of prejudice displayed by certain promoters and the French public at large who do not take EU French Caribbean artistes seriously, preferring to limit them to a kind of music which feeds into the stereotype of idle Caribbean people.[1] Schwarz-Bart believes these persistent stereotypes held by the French, resulting in their devaluing Caribbean live music, is a legacy of colonialism. He supports his belief through drawing an analogy between historical and contemporary contexts whereby present-day Caribbean artistes are commercialised as mere buffoons in the same way their enslaved ancestors were forced to entertain their colonisers as jesters (Delhaye 2018).

Other EU French Caribbean peers of Schwarz-Bart such as the celebrated Martiniquan jazz pianist Mario Canonge share the sentiment that French Caribbean live music is systemically undervalued in metropolitan France. Canonge, like Schwarz-Bart also has earned the respect of international collaborators in the United States, however when it comes to exporting his services to mainland France, he deduces that he is being blocked. Canonge describes that despite all his achievements he is labelled as nothing more than a French Caribbean musician. He also bemoans the underrepresentation of EU French Caribbean performers at festivals in mainland France (Delhaye 2018).

Guadeloupean pianist Alain-Jean Marie also echoes the views of his compatriots from the overseas French territories of the Caribbean. He also notes the underrepresentation of artistes from the EU French Caribbean at festivals in Europe, citing as an example, the marked absence of EU French Caribbean jazz artistes at many popular live jazz events in mainland France during the summer of 2018 (Delhaye 2018).

The flutist Magic Malik, originally born in Cote D'Ivoire but raised in Guadeloupe, in sharing the plight of Caribbean live music artistes in trading their services in Mainland France, describes that in France, French Caribbean jazz artistes are boxed into the Caribbean Jazz scene and have no possibility of attaining national acclaim because of their origin (Delhaye 2018).[2]

The impact of race on live music trade also appears pertinent to the independent Anglophone Caribbean context. A few have proffered that Jamaica's most prolific live music icon, Bob Marley, who was once unknown, only grew in international popularity because of his half-white ancestry. This is the belief held by Miguel Lorne, lawyer, for Bunny Wailer (one of the founding members of the Jamaican group, Bob Marley and the Wailers). Lorne argues that the British founder of Island Records, Peter Blackwell, prioritised marketing Bob Marley over his band mates Peter Tosh and Bunny Wailer because Blackwell found that Marley's half Caucasian ancestry made him an easier sell to European markets (Gardener 2022).

Although Lorne did not specify whether he was referring to Marley's physical appearance when he made this comment, it would seem that indeed the physical appearance of Caribbean live performers is taken into consideration when it comes to the international trade of their services. Alexandra Burke, a second-generation Jamaican émigré in Britain, also spoke of her experiences of being told that her complexion was too dark for the music industry and of being advised to alter her skin tone with cosmetic bleach (Pinnock 2021). Leigh-Ann Pinnock, equally a live performer of mixed Caribbean ancestry in Britain (her mother is half Barbadian and her father half Jamaican) has questioned whether her light skin won her extra privileges in the music industry over her darker peers. She has also questioned why her darker skinned peers were not considered as being commercially viable (Pinnock 2021).

Across the pond in the United States, live performers like Barbadian, Rihanna, or Cardi-B whose both parents are from CARIFO-RUM countries (Trinidad & Tobago and the Dominican Republic) have been the source of constant cyber-debates on whether their light skin won them more marketability privileges over their darker peers in the music industry. Similarly, Jamaican dancehall artiste Spice, who came under scrutiny for the transformation of her appearance from being ebony complected to being a few shades significantly lighter, spoke to the pressures imposed by the international music industry as being the cause for her decision to bleach her skin, in her song "Black Hypocrisy" (Kerr 2021). The pressures to conform to European standards of beauty, as expressed by Caribbean female artistes like Spice, are supported by scholars who have concluded that "Black women who do not meet the established standards of European beauty, are more likely to be unemployed than those who have preferred European physical characteristics (Robinson-Moore 2008 as cited in Bryant 2019)."

Light-skinned contemporary Caribbean male artistes have also been accused of being unfairly favoured over their darker hued counterparts when it comes to the commercialisation of their music. Critics have argued that Jamaican artistes Shaggy and Sean Paul, who are both of light complexion owe their commercial success to their appearance. Sean Paul, it has been argued, has had more commercial success than Mr Vegas, who is equally talented, because his (Paul's) appearance was more in line with the Eurocentric ideals of beauty.[3] There might be some merit to this assessment given that gifted and popular Jamaican Dancehall artiste Vybz Kartel, not only bleached his skin but also brought out a skin bleaching cosmetic line.

Indeed, the above examples present a compelling case for the inclusion of race and ethnicity as variables to be included for further empirical studies on their impact on Caribbean live music trade, especially when it would appear that the impact of race on live music trade does not seem to be a problem unique to Caribbean live music stakeholders but to those of other origins, as shall be seen in the next section.

The Global Problem of Race and Ethnicity on Live Music Trade

Live entertainers, owing to the nature of their profession, are called to maintain higher standards when it comes to their physical appearance. It is said to be part and parcel of the packaging strategy for the export of their services. However, it would appear, that for people of colour, this attention to the presentation of their physical appearance, comes with an enormous price. Live performers of colour, it is said, must conform to Eurocentric standards of beauty, or failing this, forfeit their hope of success in the commercialisation of their music, inclusive of their touring opportunities. The Western standards of beauty, it would seem, make it difficult for people of colour to break into European and North American markets or even within their interregional markets. This dilemma, some argue, is symptomatic of a bigger issue: The lasting effects of European colonialism or imperialism on universal perceptions of beauty. These historical Western systems which, some historians have said were designed to keep societies of colour in "their place" so that they would not feel empowered to stage uprisings, trafficked the biased notion that black was not beautiful. There are some sociologists who have analysed that the effects of these historical institutions are still felt today, given that it is universally thought that if standards of European beauty are not met, the likelihood of being passed over for employment is greater (Robinson-Moore 2008).

South Korea might be a fitting example of the effects which Western imperialist views of race and ethnicity have had on the commercialisation of live music. It is claimed, for example, that plastic surgery and skin bleaching are common among both male and female K-pop performers in an effort to attain Caucasian features such a wide-eyes, high nose bridges and light skin (Valge and Hinsberg 2019). The high frequency of appearance altering procedures among K-pop performers is theorised to be representative of the East Asian outlook that places a high premium on Caucasian features to increase employment prospects (Nakao 1993).[4] South Korea is rated as being the number one country in the world for having the highest per capita rates of plastic surgeries (Valge and Hinsberg 2019).

Interestingly, in Europe, live entertainers who come from West African diaspora communities within Northern countries, face similar pressures. Malian French artiste Aya Nakamura, for example, explained that an artistic director asked her to bleach her skin so that she could increase consumer demand for her music (Fanen 2020).

The above examples, though useful, might not be entirely representative of the big picture of how race and ethnicity affect live music trade for people of colour around the world. The above examples speak to how race and ethnicity have influenced the live music industry in terms of universal beauty standards. However, certain experts have also pointed out that the negative effects of race and ethnicity on the development of trade in Caribbean live music is not just manifested by the pressures for Caribbean artistes to conform to Eurocentric standards of beauty but also through unacknowledged cultural appropriation by countries of the North. This will be discussed in the next section.

Cultural Appropriation: An Example of the Effects of Race and Ethnicity on Caribbean Live Music Trade

Caribbean performers and producers have described how intellectually violated they have felt, when they observe that the rhythms and melodies they have crafted are repackaged and commercialised under the banner of another foreign artiste. Oftentimes the artiste is either White or a person of colour of another ethnicity. Quite often, the national origin of the artiste of colour is either European or North American. Caribbean performers who have lodged these complaints of what they consider intellectual property theft, have cited examples such as Canadian performer Justin Bieber. Bieber's chart topping single "Sorry", many would agree, clearly borrowed from Caribbean rhythms. Yet, Caribbean artistes have observed that no credit was given to the region. This has therefore stimulated debate on whether this is an instance of Caribbean cultural appropriation based on a racist system which discourages giving due credit to Caribbean creatives because of their colour and/or country of origin. Others have questioned whether international recording companies, when appropriating the music of Caribbean artistes make the conscious decision to rebrand Caribbean music under the banner of a White artiste instead of one from the Caribbean because it may result in increased consumer demand.

However, this theory, though worthy of further investigation can be challenged given that there are instances of cultural appropriation of Caribbean music by people of colour who have no regional affiliation with the Caribbean. Here the question of ethnicity rather than race, comes into play. This form of cultural appropriation suggests that international business organisations within the music industry have concluded that it is an easier sell to repackage and rebrand the catchy melodies and verses of Caribbean artistes under people of colour from North America and Europe, rather than the original Caribbean creators of the music who have produced their music within their home countries. Canadian hip hop artiste Drake, whose successful singles like "Controlla" and "One Dance" which were arguably lifted from Jamaican dancehall rhythms, was called out by Jamaican dancehall artiste Mr Vegas for Caribbean cultural appropriation. Mr Vegas challenged that the international music industry practises ethnic discrimination against Caribbean live performers whose music is home produced (Darden 2016). He expressed this view during a podcast with popular American radio host Ebro Darden:

> *When a Drake, or a Rihanna or anyone who has a big machine behind them, a Justin Bieber make a dancehall record it goes to the top...when a dancehall record is from Jamaica and we take it to other markets outside of New York, Hartford and maybe Miami, we have a problem to get it on. If you are going to come this culture (Jamaican music) put (it) on properly and give them (Jamaican artistes) an opportunity to create a name for themselves outside of their base market. What is so wrong with giving some proper crediting?*
>
> (Mr Vegas 2016 as cited in Darden 2016).

This commentary made by Mr Vegas on the unacknowledged appropriation of Caribbean music by white and black artistes from North America, suggests that there is perhaps need for empirical research on whether there is indeed a systemic problem of racism and ethnic discrimination that might be inhibiting the trade of authentically

Caribbean live music into extra-regional markets. In addition, if indeed the findings of scientific research of this nature show that race and ethnicity have a negative impact on Caribbean live music trade, there would be need for further research on the causes of why this is occurring. The following section, therefore, serves to provide more context on why race and ethnicity might be having a negative impact on Caribbean live music trade.

The Invisible Hierarchy of People of Colour: The Cause of Racism and Ethnic Prejudice against Caribbean Live Music Stakeholders

If anyone has seen the 2004 film *Hotel Rwanda*, one would be familiar with a specific dialogue between a UN peace keeping soldier played by American White actor Nick Nolte and the Rwandan hero of the movie Paul Rusesabagina portrayed by Black American actor Don Cheadle. During that key exchange, Paul expresses that he lives in hope that Rwanda would receive immediate military aid by Northern countries to put an end to the country's ethnic genocide. However, the UN peacekeeper bluntly tells Paul that he does not expect Rwandans would receive any help because of their race (black) and ethnicity (African). The crudeness in which Nolte's character uses the n-word to express his doubt about Rwandans receiving any international military aid from the North because of their being Black Africans, would be disturbing to many but in the context of live music stakeholders from the Caribbean, who are often Black, could the assessment made by Nolte's character on how the West views Black people, be applicable? Is it that within Northern countries there is the tendency to devalue Black artistes and their music? Is there a tendency to only laud Black music if it is sung and produced by Whites? Is there also the habit of only promoting a selected few of Black artistes so long as they fit the vision of those who manage large scale entertainment organisations?

In Northern countries such as France, artistes of colour observe that very little premium is accorded to Black music (inclusive of Caribbean music) by cultural institutions. Consequentially, commercial live music opportunities for Black live performers in Europe, such as those from the Caribbean, are limited. Among these European cultural institutions which accord very little recognition to the artistry of Black live music creatives is the French media. Furthermore, seemingly, the French media is particularly biased against the live music services of stakeholders from the overseas French Caribbean territories. A clear example of the French media's bias against the Overseas

French Caribbean live performers, was seen in the coverage of world-class, Guadeloupean band Kassav'. In late 2010, Kassav' staged one of its most successful concerts yet, at the prestigious Zenith stadium in Paris. The event drew scores of concertgoers who filled the stadium to its full capacity. Yet, despite, the grand success of Kassav's live music event, the French media, it was reported, presented a false narrative of the event. The media gave priority to giving a glowing coverage of French rock band Indochine, who held a live concert at the Zenith, three months after Kassav's event. The media, in unanimous fashion, fallaciously declared that Indochine was the first band to fill the Zenith stadium to its full capacity (Gomez 2011).

It is inequity in media coverage like this, which convinces Caribbean live music stakeholders, and Black artistes, in general, that they are seen as inferior, as described by Nick Nolte's character in Hotel Rwanda, because of their race. Moreover, the prejudice, it is said, is even felt more acutely by Caribbean live performers because it is believed that Northern countries perceive them as among the ethnic groups having the least value in the invisible hierarchy for people of colour. In the case of live music stakeholders from the EU French Caribbean, some have attributed their supposed low classification in this colour hierarchy, to the hybridity of their European status. Neither foreigner, nor truly being accepted as French, the treatment of EU French Caribbean live performers can be likened to the proverbial "tragic mulatto". They find no place in the White or Black music industry, despite being a product of both. Manuel Mondesir, an executive of a French Caribbean label, perhaps best describes this state of limbo that EU French Caribbean live performers find themselves in the music industry of mainland France:

> We, those of French West Indian origin, with respect to music, as in other areas, are neither in nor out. We are not classified in the category of French pop, yet we are not able to break into the world music genre.
>
> (Gomez 2011)

The above example suggests that there is an institutional system in place, either imposed deliberately or unwittingly, that limits live music trade development for Caribbean artistes of the French Caribbean within Europe. French Caribbean artistes are aggrieved that though they perform music which is a mélange of reggae, folk and acoustic guitar sounds, all of which are elements of the highly commercialised and mainstream French pop genre, they are not recognised at live music award shows nor booked for live festivals in France. Guadeloupean innovator of zouk music, the late Jacob Desvarieux, one of the founders of the legendary Guadeloupean band Kassav' decried the lack of diversity at les Victoires de la musique awards show held in 2020. Les Victoires, a music award event created by France's Ministry of Culture, is France's equivalent of the American Grammy Awards ceremony organised by the American Recording Academy. Desvarieux, normally known for his reticence and peaceful demeanour, uncharacteristically spoke out against what he observed as the promotion of systemic racism by the Les Victoires organisers.[5] He spoke out against the lack of racial diversity in the selection of nominees, he objected to the fact that the French pop category omitted the inclusion of nominees of colour, he also decried the all-White composition of the les Victoires board of judges, and he even seized the opportunity during his criticism of the Les Victoires, to point out the habitual lack of diversity of artistes slated to perform at French music festivals (Desvarieux 2020). Desvarieux's public missive to Les Victoires in which he called them out for their lack of racial diversity at their 2020 award ceremony is translated in English below[6]:

It's difficult for me because I am not normally the kind of guy who argues (...) I hardly ever argue. But come on now, don't fool us. We (Kassav') won the Les Victoires 32 years ago. We told ourselves we'll try to win it again. But no, it's no longer possible. Now, it's not even a question of the quality (of our music), or whether people listen to us...It is more a question of perhaps, someone decided that perhaps it (the award show) was too coloured and it was necessary to return to something more white (...) And you know, the thing is that when Foulquier conceptualized the Francofolies, he did it because French pop music was disappearing...now today (you're telling me) we must only have that! (the French pop music category)...Unless if they, (Les Victoires members) believe that what we're doing is not French pop music... They (Les Victoires members) have done away with the categories of World Music, they have done away with Urban Music...even in terms of the selection of judges, they have done it in such a way that they are only White. Look, I understand it (France) is a country where 99 percent of the population is White. That said, the music that one listens to is not 99 percent White. In any case, it's not a big deal. Let's leave things the way they are. That will give us the drive to create our own award ceremony for our own artistes. At least, that way, we will get exposure, and while we're at it, we'll create our own music festivals because when you see the number of

artistes from overseas French territories at festivals in mainland
France, it's a dessert...

(Desvarieux 2020)

A key organiser of the Les Victoires awards ceremony in 2020, Romain
Vivien, argued against claims by Desvarieux and others of racial discrimination in the selection of nominees. Vivien did so by explaining
that the judges' choices were merely reflective of the judges' prefer-
ences (Oliver 2020). However as journalist (Oliver 2020) points out,
this statement by Vivier is arguably a sign of "institutional racism".
Therefore, based on Desvarieux's missive and comments made by
other EU French Caribbean artistes who have expressed their difficulties in being recognised as legitimate musicians in mainland France,
one cannot help but question if their plight is a manifestation of systemic racism within the music industry of Northern countries. It just
might be, at least based on anecdotal accounts which shall be referenced in the next section.

Systemic Racism in the European Music Industry:
A reason for why trade in Caribbean Live Music is
underdeveloped.

UK newspaper, the Guardian, in a scandalously crushing report on
systemic racism in France's music industry, provided evidence that
appears to support why Caribbean artistes might be finding it difficult
to trade their services within Europe. The damning report detailed
how music statistical organisations were openly and purposefully limiting the commercial popularity of French Black artistes. One such
institution accused of this effort was the SNEP; a company in charge
of tabulating the charts and allocating royalties (Oliver 2020). It is said
that SNEP openly expressed in their 2019 report, its alarm over the tremendous popularity of rap music in France, and explicitly registered
its concern that rap's immense popularity was eclipsing the commercial attractiveness of other musical genres (Oliver 2020). In response
to what SNEP implied as the crisis of the domination of Black music
in France, SNEP strategised to reduce rap's popularity in this European country.[7] SNEP adopted a new form of calculation of streams.
Whereas previously, SNEP used to calculate both subscription and
non-subscription streams, in 2018, the organisation announced that
they would only be giving consideration to subscribed streams in
their calculations (Oliver 2020). On the other side of the coin, some
of the French music hierarchy may argue that racism against Blacks

has nothing to do with efforts to reduce the popularity of French rap but instead to curb the culture of violence and misogyny, which they perceive accompanies rap music. Former French president, Nicolas Sarkozy, for example, made an impassioned call for the boycott of French rap music because he saw it as an instrument being used to stoke violence and anti-white racism. His rallying call for limiting the popularity of French rap music found support among over 200 parliamentarians who concluded that French rap music played a key role in inciting the French riots of 2005 (Oliver 2020).

All in all, despite the changes in statistical tabulations by the SNEP, French rap continues to remain the dominant music in France, and consequentially, certainly offering to the live music stakeholders of this genre, who are mostly of either West, Central and North African ancestry, an opportunity to trade their services within France and its European environs. Therefore, based on the above accounts which suggest institutional efforts to limit the commercialisation of Black music in Europe, it is not unfathomable that Caribbean live music stakeholders would assume that such an approach to suppress rap music would extend to their music, as they too, are people of colour.

There are even those who consider that efforts to stymie the development of trade in Black music in Europe is not uniquely a French problem but possibly a general problem within countries of the European Union. Their concerns might have merit given that Caribbean academics from CARIFORUM countries have concluded that the market access provisions of the EU-CARIFORUM Economic Partnership Agreement are disproportionately skewed in favour of the EU. They base this assumption on the fact that CARIFORUM cultural practitioners might not benefit from borderless market access to the extent that EU countries would be able to within the CARIFORUM, given that CARIFORUM countries signed on as a regional trading bloc whereas the EU signed on as individual countries. Moreover, other Caribbean scholars have claimed that the Economic Needs Tests (ENTs) conditions within this agreement make it a politically correct tool for EU member states to control the number and the kind of Caribbean live music service providers who enter their territories. However, there might be some who would argue that the ENTs are being used as a polite way for the EU to safeguard their borders from criminal elements and indigents who may wish to overstay their time. Conversely, the prohibition of cross-border trade within this agreement, might serve as a telling indication of EU's desire to practice a politically correct form of cultural protectionism that some might interpret as racial and/or ethnic discrimination, that is, hurting trade for

Caribbean live music services. Findings of the Gordon (2021) study, for example, showed that the prohibition of cross-border trade in culture within the EU-CARIFORUM Economic Partnership Agreement was impacting negatively on live music services trade between EU French Caribbean territories and Anglophone CARIFORUM countries. Another point of view regarding the prohibition of cross-border cultural services trade in the agreement is that it is essential for Europeans to safeguard their culture. But within a democratic system how far should one go without infringing on the rights of consumers? Undoubtedly this issue on cross-border trade prohibitions with the EU-CARIFORUM Economic Partnership Agreement requires further debate and further research.

Conclusion

Exploring the impact of race and ethnicity on trade in Caribbean live music might be considered as either being taboo or unpopular by some. After all, why should live music which is synonymous with fun, and enjoyment be linked to such a sombre topic as racial discrimination. However, the experiences shared by some Caribbean live music stakeholders of their difficulties in trading their services in the North, which they largely attribute to their race and ethnicity, should not be ignored. Moreover, there are systemic indicators which suggest that their experiences might not be imagined. Therefore, despite how entertaining live music is perceived as being, it would be remiss of researchers to refuse to investigate whether there is validity to the concerns expressed by members of a group who feel that they are being deprived of trading opportunities because of the way they look or where they come from. Consequently, it is strongly being advised that for future studies on international trade in Caribbean live music services, that the factors of race and ethnicity be included within an empirical research design.

Notes

1 Schwarz-Bart uses a French Creole term "Doudouisme" to sum up what he perceives the stereotypical assumptions that promoters and the public of mainland France have of people from the EU French Caribbean. The author because of being proficient in both French and French creole was able to understand what was meant by this word and convey the context in which it was being used in the body of the text. See Delhaye (2018) for more details.

2 Author's translation of Magic Malik's comment in French as seen in Delhaye (2018) reads as follows: "In France, an Antillean Jazz man is

boxed into the Caribbean Jazz scene. He has no possibility of attaining national acclaim when he comes from a colony."

3 See Kerr (2021) for article titled "Sean Paul Opens Up about 'Colorism' in Dancehall and Talks Work Ethics."

4 Asian American professor Judy Yung is quoted as saying the following in a Telegram and Gazette article:

> For Asian Americans, who are flocking in growing numbers to cosmetic surgeons in search of rounder eyes and taller noses, the message is the same. It's telling them that if they want to make it in this society they have to do something about their facial features and their build.
>
> (Nakao 1993)

5 The author can attest to the characteristically laid-back demeanour of the late Jacob Desvarieux, having interviewed him for the study on live music trade between the EU French Caribbean and Anglophone CARIFORUM, and subsequently becoming friends with him. The soft-spoken Desvarieux, was considered an artiste who did not court controversy and had been interviewed by French Catholic station KTO TV to discuss his faith and its impact on his successful career in music.

6 The author translated this interview in English. The original interview published by France Televisions is in French and can be accessed through the link: (3) Watch|Facebook.

7 SNEP declared in their 2019 report that rap music is an "overexposed phenomenon" and argued that "fan support for urban music must not eclipse the performance of other musical genres (Oliver 2020)."

References

Bryant, Susan L. 2019. "The Beauty Ideal: The Effects of European Standards of Beauty on Black Women." *Columbia Social Work Review* 4: 80–91.

Darden, Ebro. 2016. "Mr Vegas Explains His Feelings on Drake." *Ebro in the Morning.* New York: Hot 97, (16th May). https://www.youtube.com/watch?v=VI-6eE_XKnE.

Delhaye, Eric. 2018. "Le jazz francais discrimine -t-il les musiciens antillais?" *Telerama*, April 25. https://www.telerama.fr/musique/le-jazz-francais-discrimine-t-il-les-musiciens-antillais,n5621362.php.

Desvarieux, Jacob, interview by N. Sarfati, N. Bensmail and M. Boscher. 2020. *Jacob Desvarieux pousse un coup de guele contre les Victoires de la musique* France Televisions. 17 January. https://www.facebook.com/watch/?v=1001853210186985.

Fanen, Sophian. 2020. "Racisme dans la musique: la revolte branche le son." *Les Jours,* 16 July.

Gardener, Claudia. 2022. "Blackwell Addresses Perceived Favoritism towards Bob Marley at The Expense of Peter Tosh, Bunny Walier." *DANCEHALL-MAG*, 30 May. https://www.dancehallmag.com/2022/05/30/news/blackwell-addresses-perceived-favoritism-towards-bob-marley-at-the-expense-of-peter-tosh-bunny-wailer.html.

Gomez, Francois-Xavier. 2011. "Antilles: Decollage Sans Media." *Libera-tion*, 4 March: 1–4. https://www.liberation.fr/musique/2011/03/04/antilles-decollage-sans-medias_719131/.

Gordon, Lisa. 2021 (Submitted). *Doctoral Thesis: The Trade in Live Music Ser-vices between European Union French Caribbean Territories and Anglophone CARIFORUM Countries: The Case Study of Guadeloupe and Trinidad & Tobago.* St Augustine: The University of The West Indies, St Augustine Campus.

Kerr, Anna-Kaye. 2021. "Sean Paul Opens Up About 'Colorism' in Dance-hall & Talks Work Ethics." *Urbanislandz*, 4 July. https://urbanislandz.com/2021/07/04/sean-paul-opens-up-about-colorism-in-dancehall-talks-work-ethics/#:~:text=Dancehall%20%2F%20Feature%20%2F%20News-,Sean%20Paul%20Opens%20Up%20About%20'Colorism,In%20Dancehall%20%26%20Talks%20Work%20Ethics&text=The%20idea.

Lazear, Edward P. 2015. "Gary Becker's Impact on Economics and Policy." *American Economic Review* 105: 80–84.

Nakao, Annie. 1993. *Telegram & Gazette*, 02 May.

Oliver, Michael. 2020. "You're Not Welcome : Rap's Racial Divide in France." *The Guardian*, 22 April. https://www.theguardian.com/music/2020/apr/22/rap-music-racial-divide-france.

Pinnock, Leigh-Anne. 2021. *Leigh-Anne: Race, Pop & Power.* Prod. BBC 3. 13 May. https://www.bbc.co.uk/iplayer/episode/p09fy1qy/leighanne-race-pop-power.

Robinson-Moore, C. L. 2008. "Beauty Standards Reflect Eurocentric Paradigms—So What? Skin Color, Identity, and Black Female Beauty." *The Journal of Race & Policy* (Norfolk) 4: 66–85.

Valge, Claudia and Maari Hinsberg. 2019. "The Capitalist Control of K-Pop: The Idol as a Product." *ICDS Diplomaatia*, 2 October. https://icds.ee/en/the-capitalist-control-of-k-pop-the-idol-as-a-product/.

Wright, Jack. 2022. "Sir Lenny Henry Questions Diversity at Glastonbury." *Mail Online*, 14 June.

ZEE News. 2013. *British Indian Musician Alleges Racism at Glastonbury Festival.* 23 June. https://zeenews.india.com/news/world/british-indian-musician-alleges-racism-at-glastonbury-festival_857158.html.

8 Implications of Technology, Legal Institutions, and Geographic Proximity in the Development of Trade in Caribbean Live Music

Technology for the Development of Trade in Caribbean Live Music Services

In the Gordon (2021) study conducted on live music services trade between the overseas Caribbean territories of France and independent Anglophone countries of the Caribbean, it was revealed that technology had a positive impact on this trade.[1] However, the descriptive data painted a different picture. It showed that technology was trending negatively for live music services trade between these two Caribbean sub-regions.[2] Therefore, it was important to find out what could have been accounting for this variance in the data. In delving deeper into the findings, it was discovered that live music stakeholders from both the EU French Caribbean and Anglophone independent CARIFO-RUM territories believed that technology was not being adequately harnessed for the development of international trade within their region. Hence, by examining how South Korea has successfully used technology for the development of international trade in live K-pop music, one can then analyse whether South Korea's example could be a viable option for the advancement of international trade in Caribbean live music services.

In services trade, the use of technology has been traditionally associated with cross-border economic activity between countries, through ICT (mode 1). Therefore, economic exchanges in services via telecommunications, satellite, and the internet are media through which cross-border trade is supported. In the case of live music, cross-border trade was not traditionally associated with this service. This is because live music services are customarily traded when consumers travel to events (mode 2) and when artistes tour (mode 4). However, the early 2000's and beyond have heralded new ICT inventions, with research and development in ICT currently on the rise. Therefore,

DOI: 10.4324/9781003343325-8

the Caribbean should not drop the ball in using technology for the advancement of its live music services, in light of the continued scientific efforts to expand the usefulness of technology by multinational companies. The following section, therefore, looks into the South Korean strategy of using technology for the development of international trade in its live music. Again, South Korea has been referenced because of the astounding success in the international commercialisation of its entertainment services, like live music.

How South Korea Has Capitalised on Technology to Develop International Trade in Live Music

South Koreans have been taking full advantage of advancements in ICT since the early 2000s for the development of trade in entertainment services such as live music. Since YouTube was launched in 2005, South Korea might be arguably among the precursors which have used this platform to develop international trade in their entertainment services. Live music artistes from this East Asian country have been using this platform for the purpose of exposing potential intraregional consumers (Japan and China) as well as extra-regional markets (Europe and the United States), to K-pop music. Who can forget the viral international success of K-pop artiste, Psy's "Gangnam Style", when it was uploaded to YouTube back in December 2012? The video which garnered over a billion views provided K-pop with the international exposure which would have surely contributed to potential consumers acquiring a taste for K-pop live music.

Contemporary South Korean bands like BTS, continue to apply this strategy of using technology for capturing new international fans. K-pop artistes have successfully attracted a fan-base in EU countries such as France, thanks to their use of social-media distribution channels (Oh and Sung-Park 2012). Content distribution channels like YouTube, Tik Tok, and Instagram are widely used as a way to attract both intraregional and extra-regional netizens. It is a brilliant strategy that is also being applied by other regions such as Africa. It is hard to forget the 2020 viral sensation created by South Africans Master KG and Nomcebo when their single "Jerusalema" was uploaded on YouTube. On YouTube their single attracted over 515 million views and spawned a variety of dance memes from across the globe which were viewed via social network platforms like TikTok.

The South Korean approach of investing heavily in social media and content platforms for increasing international demand for its entertainment services, illustrates that its strategic vision involves using cross-border mediums (mode 1) to create touring opportunities for its artistes (mode 4) and increase the number of festival tourists (mode 2). This strategy seems to be working. It was reported, for example, that when Germany, held KPOP.FLEX back in May 14–15, 2022, it was estimated that the two-day live music event drew 80,000 K-pop fans from all over Europe (Yonhap News Agency 2022). These numbers are impressive especially when one considers the imposed two-year live music hiatus within EU countries and the rest of the world because of the COVID-19 pandemic. The success of this event indicates that even during the pandemic, South Korea heavily invested on using social media and content platforms to sustain the viability of its live music industry.

The South Korean Technology Strategy – A Viable Approach for Trade in Caribbean Live Music?

Can this South Korean strategy of heavily investing on social media and content platforms be also effective in the development of trade in Caribbean live music services? It can, provided that it is done shrewdly. Currently many Caribbean artistes use platforms like YouTube to make themselves discoverable by potential live music consumers. However, findings from the Gordon (2021) study on live music trade between EU French Caribbean territories and Anglophone CARI-FORUM countries showed that the volume of trade is low between the two regions. Therefore, it suggests that the benefits being accrued through content platforms for K-pop artists have not been as profitable for live music artistes from the Caribbean. Perhaps it has to do with the fact that South Korean live music stakeholders are using the platforms differently to those in the Caribbean (Oh and Sung-Park 2012), for example, in explaining why there is a significant demand for K-pop live music in France, referenced how French fans discovered K-pop content through online and offline Asian cultural hubs. This suggests that South Korean entertainment companies, when upload-ing the videos of their artistes, strategically ensure that the uploaded content is accessible to online social media hubs comprising of fans of East Asian culture, who might also be members of associations which celebrate East Asian culture. This South Korean strategy could be one that might yield profitable results for live music Caribbean stake-holders. Online English-speaking Caribbean cultural hubs in the non-sovereign Caribbean States and their respective European metropoles could be created or located for the purpose of exposing their popu-lations to music from the English-speaking Caribbean. In 2022, the

Organisation of Eastern Caribbean States in partnership with the International Organisation of Migration completed a study to locate Caribbean diaspora populations in North America. Their findings located several Caribbean diaspora associations across North American cities. The database from that study could be used for the purpose of reaching out to these Caribbean diaspora populations to mobilise the creation of online hubs for Caribbean culture or locate online hubs which the diaspora already frequent. These Caribbean diaspora associations especially in North America and Europe, might also provide leads on non-Caribbean diaspora friends or acquaintances who are fans of Anglo-Caribbean culture. However, prior to implementing the South Korean strategy of using technology for the development of international trade in Caribbean live music services, experimental studies should first be conducted.

Legal Institutions and Trade in Caribbean Live Music Services

Legal institutions are not having a significant nor positive impact on trade in live music services between sovereign and non-sovereign Caribbean territories. These were the empirical findings from the Gordon (2021) experimental study on trade in live music services between EU French Caribbean territories and Anglophone CARIFORUM countries, following regression analysis.[3] These findings were not surprising because the comparative descriptive statistics provided a more complete picture of why legal institutions were negatively impacting on interregional trade in Caribbean live music services. Overall music stakeholders from the Anglophone CARIFORUM and specifically Trinidad & Tobago rate their legal institutions more negatively than those of the EU French Caribbean territories.[4] However, EU French Caribbean respondents had an optimistic view of their legal framework.

These findings, therefore, offer a more complete picture of the legal institutional environment of the Caribbean region, with the independent anglophone live music stakeholders being dissatisfied with the legal frameworks within which they are obliged to operate, and the non-sovereign territories being relatively satisfied with their legal institutions. These differences in levels of confidence between sovereign and non-sovereign territories regarding their respective legal frameworks might portend potential trade disputes. Indeed, conflicting legal frameworks between the regions suggest that one territory is offering a level of protection for the rights of its artistes that is not enjoyed in the other territory, and such conditions are never good for trade. Therefore, to address this issue, there is need to implement initiatives for harmonising laws to facilitate both South-South and North-South interregional trade in Caribbean live music services. The next section proposes how this can be done.

A Proposed Solution to Harmonising Laws to Favour International Trade in Caribbean Live Music

A system is already set up that favours this kind of legal harmonisation. The OHADAC Regional Arbitration Centre (under the acronym CARO) is an interregional organisation which was founded for the purpose of harmonising commercial and civil laws of both sovereign and non-sovereign Caribbean territories.[5] The CARO Centre which is financed by the European Union, began its operations in the Caribbean in September 2021. In its thrust towards the harmonisation of commercial law in the region, the CARO centre launched in 2021 its first set of arbitration and mediation procedures through setting up the recourse facility known as Alternative Dispute Resolution (ADR). The principal purpose of ADR is to provide mediation and arbitration services to business parties as they hold ongoing negotiations on contractual arrangements. The ADR facility therefore provides legally trained mediators who intervene from the start of business negotiations to the time of completion of a project. These mediators oversee contractual arrangements from start to finish, and identify loopholes which they assess could be a source of contention between business parties. This kind of mediation serves as a pre-emptive measure to stave off possible legal disputes before they occur.

It is therefore being proffered that with respect to interregional trade in Caribbean live music services that the CARO centre be used as an institution to intervene in negotiations between live music stakeholders who hail from Caribbean territories of different geopolitical contexts and consequently different legal frameworks. The mediators who intervene on CARO's behalf should be experts in intellectual property law of the Commonwealth and the European Union given that the Caribbean region follows either of these legal frameworks. Similarly, these mediation services offered by the CARO would also be useful to North-South extra-regional trade in live music services between the independent CARIFORUM and the European Union. However, prior to implementing this project, there would be need to conduct a preliminary audit to confirm if the human capital is available to initiate such a project. Ideally, this human capital should comprise of competent bilingual legal professionals versed in intellectual property law of the Caribbean as well as that of Europe and North America. Equally, empirical studies should be conducted to collect and analyse primary data sourced from the regions' live music stakeholders. This exercise will help the CARO determine how best to implement this project.

Geographic Proximity and South-South Interregional Trade in Caribbean Live Music

Geographic Proximity or (closeness) between countries is revealed as the factor having the most significant and positive impact on interregional trade in Caribbean live music services. This finding was revealed in the Gordon (2021) experimental study on trade in live music services between the overseas Caribbean territories of France and the independent English-Speaking Caribbean.[6] Notwithstanding this result from the Gordon (2021) study, the descriptive data from that same study did not align with this finding. The descriptive data showed that despite the geographic closeness between sovereign and non-sovereign Caribbean territories, live music stakeholders from both subregions believed that South-South interregional trade in live music services was trending negatively.[7] They blamed the lack of connectivity in both marine and air-transport, the high cost of these means of transport, as well as the geopolitical differences between sovereign and non-sovereign Caribbean territories as the cause for why despite the geographic proximity between the territories, South-South interregional trade in Caribbean live music services was trending negatively.

Indeed, the fact that the empirical model which shows that geographic proximity has the most significant and positive impact on interregional trade in Caribbean live music services is at variance with the live music stakeholders' views on the matter, suggests that much work needs to be done to optimise the positive impact that the geographic closeness among the territories ought to be having on South-South interregional trade in Caribbean live music services. The next section calls for a recommitment to the project which once held the promise of resolving the issue of transportation within the Caribbean.

Re-investment in the Multi-Destination Project

The multi-destination project which has been discussed since circa 2012 held the promise of resolving the difficulties of air and marine transport in the Caribbean. The project was hailed as a solution to address the lack of competitiveness of the Caribbean region in terms of extra-regional tourism. It was believed that if the Caribbean could brand themselves as a region offering a variety of experiences at one cost, it would make the region more aggressively competitive as an amalgamated unit rather than as individual micro-territories.[8] To this end, plans were made to develop marine and air transport infrastructure among the islands and to offer air and marine transport services at affordable prices. It was also envisaged that doing away with current visa restrictions within the Caribbean would be beneficial to intraregional and extra-regional tourism, education, and research. However, since those discussions, the project has not gotten off the ground. Intraregional air and marine transport services within the CARICOM Caribbean remain unaffordable to many. Equally, interregional air and marine transport between sovereign and non-sovereign Caribbean territories is both impractical in terms of itinerary (delays, long stops, and layovers), and astronomical in terms of cost. Therefore, Caribbean leadership, the private sector, along with interested international funding organisations which have stakes in the Caribbean, should urgently see to the revival of the noble goals enounced in the multi-destination tourism project.

The revival and success of this project would no doubt be an invaluable asset to South-South interregional trade in Caribbean live music services, given that uninhibited travel within the region would be an asset for touring (mode 4) and festival tourism (mode 2). Development of this project would be equally advantageous to the development of North-South extra-regional trade in Caribbean live music via mode 2 (festival tourism). This is because for concertgoers in the North, the promise of an experience which allows them to taste the music festivals from various Caribbean destinations would be certainly attractive. The multi-destination project would be equally beneficial to artistes wishing to tour in Europe. This is because by flying in-transit through overseas-EU Caribbean territories at affordable prices, they might benefit from a less costly and time-consuming means of arriving in continental Europe. For instance, in overseas French Caribbean territories like Guadeloupe, direct return flights to Paris can cost as low as 400 euros. Interestingly, there are already some elements of the multi-destination project on stream which links the Anglophone Independent CARIFORUM with the French Caribbean and with continental Europe. The Guadeloupean air service provider Air Caraibes, for instance, has a travel itinerary that connects the citizens of Dominica to mainland France. The trip itinerary is practical because Air Caraibes organises an in-transit water-taxi between Dominica and Guadeloupe and then air transport services from Guadeloupe to France. Therefore, it is being proposed that a similar multi-modal transport system be applied to the rest of the Caribbean. This system could involve collaboration among the region's airlines and marine transport companies. Of course, there might be legal considerations to iron out, but this could certainly be facilitated by the CARO's Alternative Dispute Resolution services. However, once again, in depth experimental research should be done before implementation of this proposal.

Final Thoughts

This last chapter wraps up an enlightening journey on international trade in Caribbean live music services. The value of this book lies in the scope of issues covered, some of which might not be normally associated with international trade and others which might be considered provocative. Nonetheless, all the issues covered in this book show how pertinent they are for the development of international trade in Caribbean live music and why further empirical studies on these subject matters are required. Hopefully, this book would inspire a new generation of researchers to expand their understanding of international trade beyond their knowledge of economic theory or econometrical equations. Similarly, it is hoped that this book would awaken the curiosity of researchers, schooled in qualitative methods, to explore empirical methods for future studies on Caribbean creative and cultural industries. In this way they would contribute to the body of knowledge of this sector.

This book by tackling issues such as race and ethnicity, the unachieved regionalism of the Caribbean, the perceived biases in interregional trade arrangements between regions of the North and South, as well as the relationships that European nations have with their overseas Caribbean territories, should stimulate open and free constructive debates on topics that might have been initially, considered as taboo to discuss, particularly in relation to international trade. One envisages that through the open and free discussions generated by this book about the issues regarding international trade and live music services, consensus on how best to move forward will be established.

Finally, the proposals to incorporate foreign policy objectives as well as sustainable development initiatives, into live music trade strategies, should provide food for thought. Hopefully, this book would also be the impetus for exploring the viability of proposals made to harness diaspora populations, implement initiatives against language barriers, harmonise commercial and IP laws between regions, as well as revitalising projects for air and marine interconnectivity for both South-South and North-South interregional travel.

The future is bright for creative and cultural industries in the Caribbean region, once all interested parties work in unison. Cooperative efforts to develop international trade in Caribbean live music services between South-South and North-South parties would reap tremendous rewards for the Caribbean's at-risk youths. Youths, who though incredibly talented, have not been afforded the opportunity to export their talent to the world. Their impoverished circumstances and the stigma of their criminality are among the reasons that deprive them of this opportunity. The region and the world, however, should feel morally bound to assist, as we are all our brothers' keepers. Investing handsomely and sustainably in the development of international trade in Caribbean live music services, will be an embodiment of the spirit of global brotherhood. This investment would also be a manifestation of a collective commitment towards aspiring to the ideal, that to whom much is given, much is expected.

Notes

1 In the Gordon (2021) study examining trade in live music services between EU French Caribbean territories and Anglophone CARIFORUM countries, regression analysis revealed that similarities in technology have a positive impact on this trade. This is because the Pearson correlation value linked to this variable is .198. The study's findings also showed that technology, when compared to the other variables, has a limited degree of significance on the trade live music services between the EU French Caribbean and the Anglophone CARIFORUM. It accounted for the second lowest p-value (.063), after the variable geographic proximity, which had a p-value below the alpha −.05. It is however being acknowledged, that the p-value for technology, although being the second lowest, was nevertheless above the alpha p-value .05. It is for this reason, the impact of technology's effect on the trade between the two subregions is being described as limited.

2 The descriptive data on technology was at variance with the positive Pearson correlation value associated with this variable. Respondents from the EU French Caribbean and Anglophone CARIFORUM gave an overall low score on the impact that similarities in technology has had on live music trade, with those from the EU French Caribbean scoring this variable at 2.99 and the Anglophone CARIFORUM at 2.73. Among the reasons for their negative perception on the impact that similarities in technology has had on live music trade is that they are both dissatisfied with how their technology has been used to promote trade in live music services between the two countries.

3 The p-value associated with similarities in Legal Institutions was way above .05 with a score of .268, thus indicating that this variable is currently

not having a significant impact on this on this trade. The Pearson Correlation value also indicated that similarities in legal institutions were impacting negatively on this trade as is seen by the negative score of −081.

4 The mean score given by music stakeholders from Trinidad & Tobago, relative to this variable was 2.99 just .01 below the midpoint average 3.

5 See the website of the CARO Centre for more information on their activities CARO - The CARO Centre (carohadac.org).

6 In the Gordon (2021) study, results following regression analysis revealed that Geographic Proximity is the variable which has the most significant impact on the volume of trade in live music services between the two countries. Its t-stat co-efficient was the only one among the six variables which was above 1. In addition, its p-value read .022 which corresponded to the recommended benchmark of p-values needing to be less than .05 to predict the significance of independent variables on the dependent variables. In addition, its Pearson Correlation value was .369, which was above 0, thus indicating that the variable is having a positive impact on trade. This finding is consistent with (Rouet 2007/2015)'s study where geographic considerations like distance had a significant impact on the volume of trade in cultural services between France and its foreign trading partners. In their study, countries which were geographically closer enjoyed more favorable trading relationships whereas countries which were more distant experienced less favorable trading relationships.

7 Relative to the descriptive data in the Gordon (2021) study, which was at variance with the results from regression, the mean value for Geographic Proximity was 1.97 for each country, a negative value which is significantly below the midpoint 3 of the 5-point Likert scale. See Gordon (2021) study for more details.

8 Between 2018 and 2021, Interreg Caraibes financed the Blue Odyssea Multi-Destination Project. Since the project ended in 2021, however, the issue of inter-island connectivity persists. An outline of the objectives of the Blue Odyssea Multi-Destination Project financed by Interreg Caraibes can be found: on the Interreg Caraibes website. Le Projet ODYSSEA CARAÏBES BLUE GROWTH MULTI-DESTINATION|Projets Odyssea.

References

Gordon, Lisa. 2021 (Submitted). *Doctoral Thesis: The Trade in Live Music Services between European Union French Caribbean Territories and Anglophone CARIFORUM Countries: The Case Study of Guadeloupe and Trinidad & Tobago.* St Augustine: The University of The West Indies, St Augustine Campus.

Interreg Caraibes. 2022. *Odyssea Blue Growth Multi-Destination.* Accessed August 27, 2022. https://www.odyssea.eu/projets/programmes-europeens/projets-europeens-14-20/odyssea-caraibes-blue-growth-multi-destination/le-projet-odyssea-caraibes-blue-growth-multi-destination/#:~:text=Le%20projet%20Odyssea%20Blue%20Growth%20Multi-Destination%20est%20.

Oh, Ingyu, and Gil Sung Park. 2012. "From B2C to B2B: Selling Korean Pop Music in the New Age of Social Media." *Korea Observer* 365.

Rouet, Francois. 2007/2015. "Le flux d'echanges internationaux de biens et services culturels: determinants et enjeux." Edited by DEPS: (Departement des etudes de la prospective et des statistiques. *Culture Etudes CE-2007-1 et des Statistiques* (OpenEdition Books) CE-2007-1. doi:9782111398719.

Yonhap News Agency. 2022. "NCT DREAM Says "European K-pop Fans that We Met for the First Time Are Very Passionate"." *K-ODESSEY*, 16 May. https://k-odyssey.com/news/newsview.php?ncode=1065595871365378.

Index

Printed in the United States
by Baker & Taylor Publisher Services